SPIRIT, SON and FATHER

SPIRIT, SON and FATHER

Christian Faith in the Light of the Holy Spirit

by HENRY P. VAN DUSEN

President of Union Theological Seminary, New York, and
Roosevelt Professor of Systematic Theology

Lectures on the James A. Gray Fund
of the Divinity School of Duke University
Durham, North Carolina

ADAM & CHARLES BLACK

LONDON

THIS EDITION FIRST PUBLISHED 1960

A. AND C. BLACK LIMITED
4, 5 AND 6 SOHO SQUARE LONDON W.I

© 1958 HENRY P. VAN DUSEN

PRINTED IN THE UNITED STATES OF AMERICA

These chapters were initially given as Lectures on the James A. Gray Fund at Duke University Divinity School.

> "The James A. Gray Fund was established at the Divinity School of Duke University in 1946 as a part of the Methodist College Advance of the North Carolina Conferences of the Methodist Church. The purpose of the fund, in the words of the donor, is to expand and maintain the educational services of the Duke Divinity School in 'behalf of the North Carolina churches and pastors, particularly rural churches and pastors.'"

Subsequently, in revised and expanded form, they were delivered as:

The Chancellor Lectures,
QUEENS UNIVERSITY, ONTARIO.

The Zimmerman Lectures,
LUTHERAN THEOLOGICAL SEMINARY, GETTYSBURG.

The Carnahan Lectures,
UNION THEOLOGICAL SEMINARY, BUENOS AIRES.

A PERSONAL PREFACE

Every author owes his readers at least some explanation of how his writing came to be.

For some years now, within the whole range of Christian faith, the "Holy Spirit" has been my favorite theme.

But the Holy Spirit has been, for me, a late discovery. All early associations in my mind connected with the term were not only vague but unpleasant, indeed almost repellent. The attitudes which I have attributed to the "typical layman" in these pages were mine. For one thing, the use (as I think, tragic and indefensible *mis*use) of the phrase "Holy *Ghost*" conveyed impressions of a "something" dubious as to both reality and worth; "whatever more and other the Holy Ghost might be, it unfailingly conveyed the impression of something misty, nebulous, 'ghostly,' unattractive." These unfavorable associations were doubtless aggravated by the references to the Holy Ghost in the teaching and hymnody of the Church—"the confused metaphors of popular devotion, with its medley of doves and flames and winds and still small voices."[1]

[1] Charles E. Raven, *The Creator Spirit*, p. 1.

I cannot tell precisely when or through what influences I first began to turn toward the thought of the Holy Spirit with other than misgiving if not repugnance. As a seminary student more than thirty years ago, I attended Professor E. F. Scott's brilliant lectures, subsequently published as *The Idea of the Spirit in the New Testament*. However, I do not recall that they made any special impression upon my mind. Years later, to be sure, when I was preparing these chapters, I turned back to Dr. Scott's book to discover in it some of the most enlightening and enriching material upon which I have not hesitated to draw extensively.

Upon my shelves, I discover two well-worn and heavily marked volumes which I must have read with uncommon thoroughness in the nineteen-twenties—*The Spirit*, issued in 1921 by Canon B. H. Streeter and his colleagues of the "Cumnor Group," and *The Creator Spirit*, written by Canon C. E. Raven in 1927. I suspect that, as is so often the case, these writings lodged in my subconscious mind seeds of suggestion which, lying long fallow, eventually emerged as mature convictions.

My first exposure to the claimed "experience of the Holy Spirit" had come much earlier, in schooldays. Once a week for four years, as a pupil in a Quaker school in Philadelphia, I was compelled to sit in the old Friends Meeting-house on South Twelfth Street through an hour of boring and restive silence punctuated by intermittent and usually disjointed utterances by devout Quakers. Many years later, I was to discover that the simplicity and integrity of that imposed ordeal had pierced through the antagonistic *conscious* mind and had lodged in the *sub*consciousness gifts of genuine reality upon which I was later to draw heavily and gratefully when the lad's indifference to religion had given place to the man's intense interest, indeed preoccupation with religion. But the concept of the "guidance of the Holy Spirit" was not within that strange deposit of unintended and unrecognized indebtedness.

It was probably contact with "Buchmanism" in its earlier and far more worthy expressions (1921-1927) which first challenged me to recognize both the inescapable logic and the experienced reality of the "guidance of the Spirit." Indeed, my most lasting debt to that bafflingly ambivalent Movement is precisely an interwoven conviction and experience. The *conviction* is that, if there be a Living God at all, He must desire to make His will and purposes known to men and that a silent, receptive, expectant consciousness furnishes Him the most favorable condition for the disclosure of His thoughts to the minds of men. The *experience* has been that, when I did so take up an attitude of openminded and responsive expectancy, thoughts and ideas and directives often came which subsequent empirical testing validated as the closest approximation to trustworthy divine guidance which is available to us.

As far as I can determine, it was a suggestion from my wife which first set my mind to the attempt to discern what truth and significance might be discovered in the whole idea of the Holy Spirit. About twenty years ago, she urged, "I wish you would preach sometime on the Holy Spirit, upon the text: 'Take not Thy Holy Spirit from me.'" Long before, I had been taught in seminary classes in Homiletics that, when one finds that he is neglecting some basic concept of Christian Faith, the best cure is to compel oneself to search the Scriptures for the meanings hidden there, and then to preach upon it. And so, I discover in a folder of sermon-outlines, under date of April 25, 1937, the time-darkened notes of my first attempt to make earnest with that great and hallowed plea from the Fifty-first Psalm and the conviction of the Holy Spirit which it embodies.

The decisive factor, however, was a necessity laid upon me —the obligation, in expounding the essentials of Christian Faith in a basic course in Systematic Theology, to deal with the Doctrine of the Holy Spirit.

In the course of that agonizing exercise, I turned back to another book which had lain on my shelves for years but, so far as I can tell, up to then neglected—H. Wheeler Robinson's *The Christian Experience of the Holy Spirit*. Here, at long last, the truth concerning the Holy Spirit was made to come alive with intellectual compulsion and spiritual challenge. My indebtedness to Principal Robinson's thought is sufficiently revealed in the frequent references to his work in the pages which follow. His book is still, I believe, much the profoundest, soundest and most satisfying exposition of this neglected conviction of faith. If this little volume should serve to tempt its readers to secure and peruse his great work, I would be satisfied.

Finally, the significance of the Holy Spirit for a fuller apprehension and comprehension of the other great convictions of Christian belief is a realization which has come to me slowly and with mounting meaning over a number of years as I have sought to make convincing and compelling to generation after generation of theological students the reality which has by now become, for me, the most exciting, enlarging and enriching element in our Faith.

It is a major frustration of most academic administrators that their primary obligations allow so little opportunity for serious and sustained writing. By no means is this to suggest that they cease reading; certainly, I trust, they do not stop thinking. On the contrary, their minds play constantly on the great issues to which their earlier studies have been devoted. More often than not, their many and diversified contacts and tasks set these issues in far more comprehensive and therefore more adequate context. From time to time, illumination is given, insight clarifies, conviction crystallizes. Articles and books form in their minds and cry for recording. But—immediate duties press in upon them and demand priority. Time is lacking; there is the rub. And so a whole shelf-full of ideas accumulate in the mind, but are given neither the formulation nor the exposure to criticism which only systematic exposition and publication can make possible.

These pages are the modest fruit of many years of such brooding, reading, and reflection. They had their origin in class-room lectures in Systematic Theology. In their present form, they were prepared for successive series of lectures to ministers and lay folk. As the importance of the theme and the possibility of offering some fresh contribution to its more adequate understanding grew upon me, the hope formed of making this inquiry into the bearing of the Holy Spirit upon the other major convictions of Christian Faith the principal focus of attention for a study to be carried forward, summer by summer, over a considerable period of years, eventuating perhaps in a sizeable and not altogether unworthy treatment of so great and, as I think, neglected a subject. I still cling to that possibility as a hope. However, there appears slight prospect of an early fulfillment of that intention. Accordingly, I have decided, not without regret and misgiving, to commit these preliminary formulations to what my friend, the late

Albert Parker Fitch, used to describe as the "awful perpetuity of print." I shall continue to cling to the hope that at some later date, probably many years hence, opportunity will offer for the more comprehensive and adequate development of the material which had been intended.

My indebtedness to a very few books is suggested above and in the extended quotations from them which are incorporated in the text.

To two of my colleagues I am indebted for discerning and wise criticism of part or all of the manuscript. Professor James Muilenburg examined Chapters 2 and 3 in an early draft. Professor Cyril C. Richardson read the entire text. His modesty prevented him from revealing that his own volume on *The Doctrine of the Trinity* was ready for publication, so that, to my regret, I did not have the opportunity to see it before these chapters were in the printer's hands; I would reciprocate the comment he has generously inscribed on a complimentary copy of his book: "I should have written more wisely had I had the good fortune to read your book first."

Lastly, special and affectionate thanks go to a sequence of devoted secretaries who have copied the manuscript in its successive editions, and especially to that beloved triumvirate —Mrs. Jane Catlett Ballard, Mrs. Mary Helen Cavaghan and Mrs. Martha C. Spivey—who together produced the penultimate draft, to Mrs. Nancy Morris Grant who is responsible for the final manuscript and to Miss Gladys M. Burkhart for assistance on the Index.

H.P.V.D.

UNION THEOLOGICAL SEMINARY,
NEW YORK,
APRIL 27, 1958

CONTENTS

Part III. Spirit, Son and Father

Part IV. Conclusion

SPIRIT, SON and FATHER

To my Sister

KATHARINE PITNEY VAN DUSEN

Not by the spoken word,
  Not by the written word,
  But by the word lived,
Is the WORD OF LIFE revealed.

PROLOGUE

The formulation of our theme—"Spirit, Son, and Father"—is unfamiliar. And, at first hearing, doubtless startling. The order is, of course, deliberate. Moreover, it is fully in accord with a sound Christian orthodoxy.

Christian Faith proclaims a God Who is—"Father, Son and Holy Spirit." And the Athanasian Creed affirms:

> "The Godhead of the Father, of the Son, and of the Holy Ghost is one—the glory equal, the majesty coeternal. . . . In this Trinity none is before or after other, none is greater or less than another; but the whole three Persons are co-eternal together and co-equal."

Moreover, it is an accepted premise of Christian thought that all the major beliefs of its Faith are mutually involved and interdependent. It should be possible and legitimate to make one's start from any one of them, and approach all the others through it. Especially is this true with respect to the basic and central belief of the Faith—its conception of God.

Traditionally, Christian Theology, in setting forth its con-

3

ception of Deity, has taken its start from "God the Father Almighty, Maker of Heaven and Earth," and has then passed on to "Jesus Christ, His only Son, our Lord," and has come at last (usually at long last) to "the Holy Spirit." In this sequence, it has been faithful to the order of all the earliest creeds from the Apostles' Creed onward. These, in turn, rest back upon the final injunction of the Risen Lord as reported in the concluding words of the First Gospel:

> "Go therefore and make disciples of all nations, baptizing them in the name of the Father and of the Son and of the Holy Spirit." (Matthew 28:19)

Sometimes, however, Christian theologians have first considered Christ, and then God-in-the-light-of-Christ, and finally the Holy Spirit. For this sequence, likewise, there is strong Scriptural warrant. For the other great Triune formula, which early wove its way into the liturgy of Christians as the "Great Benediction" and has held that place through the centuries even to our own day, declares:

> "The grace of the Lord Jesus Christ and the love of God and the fellowship of the Holy Spirit be with you all." (II Corinthians 13:14)

This is the guiding principle of all "Christo-centric" theologies.

Seldom if ever has an exposition of Christian Faith made its beginning with the Holy Spirit, and then gone on to consider Christ-in-the-light-of-the-Holy-Spirit and finally God-in-the-light-of-the-Holy-Spirit. That is the experiment we are to attempt.

The late Archbishop Temple was fond of urging that

every Christian prayer might well commence rather than conclude with "Through Jesus Christ Our Lord," and then move on to one of the familiar addresses to Deity with which we customarily begin our prayers: "Almighty and Everlasting God," etc. Anyone who has taken Dr. Temple's suggestion seriously, as he intended, and has so invariably begun his prayers will bear witness to the startling correction as well as enrichment which the practice has brought to his praying.

What we are here proposing is to carry Dr. Temple's principle one step further: to begin our thought with the Holy Spirit, as though the Pauline Blessing had been phrased, "The fellowship of the Holy Spirit, and the grace of the Lord Jesus Christ, and the love of God be with you all"; or as though the Great Commission attributed to the Risen Christ had instructed His followers to baptize "in the name of the Holy Spirit, and of the Son, and of the Father"; or as though our creeds declared: "I believe in the Holy Spirit— and in Jesus Christ, our Lord—and in God the Father Almighty."

Two prior steps must prepare the way for that undertaking, however. We shall first seek answer to the query which lies latent in many minds, "Yes, but why the Holy Spirit anyhow?" We then shall attempt to clarify our thought of what is meant by the Holy Spirit by tracing the development of that conception in its long and tortuous pilgrimage through the centuries.

PART ONE

INTRODUCTION

CHAPTER I *"Why the Holy Spirit?"*

CHAPTER ONE

"WHY THE HOLY SPIRIT?"

A senior and revered leader of the contemporary church, the late Dr. H. Wheeler Robinson of Oxford, tells us that:

> "in the course of a serious illness, he was led to ask himself why the truths of 'evangelical' Christianity which he had often preached to others now failed to bring him personal strength. They remained true to him, but they seemed to lack vitality. They seemed to demand an active effort of faith, for which the physical energy was lacking. The figure that presented itself at the time was that of a great balloon, with ample lifting power,—if only one had the strength to grasp the rope that trailed down from it! . . . The result of this experience was . . . to lead him to seek for the lacuna in his own conception of evangelical truth. He found it in his relative neglect of those conceptions of the Holy Spirit in which the New Testament is so rich."[1]

A further consequence of this episode was that Dr. Robinson was spurred by it to undertake an intensive inquiry into

[1] H. Wheeler Robinson, *The Christian Experience of the Holy Spirit*, New York: Harper & Brothers, p. 4.

9

"The Christian Experience of the Holy Spirit." Fifteen years later, the fruits of his study were gathered up in the most helpful treatment of this neglected and needful theme which has been given to the Church in our time.

2.

Am I mistaken in the impression that Dr. Robinson speaks, both for not a few of us as individuals, and for our generation? And, in two respects:—

1) With many of us, his need is our need, too. The beliefs of our religion when most needed are unshaken, but they do not generate effective power. There is a gap between the convictions in our minds and their grip upon our lives. Faith and practice fail to "mesh." Could we not echo Dr. Robinson's words: "The truths of evangelical Christianity remain true, but they seem to lack vitality. They seem to demand an active effort of faith for which the energy is lacking, like a great balloon with ample lifting power, if only one had the strength to grasp the rope."? Our need, as with him, may be for physical re-enforcement in hours of weakness. Or, as with the Apostle Paul, for moral strength to master temptation and transcend failure: "The good that I would, I do not: but the evil which I would not, that I do. . . . Who shall deliver me?"[2] Or, as with the author of the Gospel of John, for guidance in perplexity and confusion, for a "Counselor," "the Spirit of truth."[3] Or, as with the Psalmist, for cleansing and remaking in the despair of devas-

[2] Romans 7:19, 24.
[3] John 14:16.

tating self-knowledge: "Have mercy on me, O God. . . . Create in me a clean heart, and renew a right spirit within me."[4] Or, in general, in our pitiful pettiness, foolishness and waywardness, for the basic essentials of character: "love, joy, peace, patience, kindness, goodness, faithfulness, gentleness, self-control."[5] Our most urgent necessity is for the "fruits of the Spirit."

Nor is this a personal lack only. In the theological thought and discussions of today, the contentions which are most clamorous and self-assured—whether neo-orthodox or neo-Reformation or neo-Calvinist or neo-whatever—may convince the mind; they often fail to change the person. Something is lacking, and that which is lacking is what is most important. They promise and produce no adequate alteration of life—that redirection of purpose and transformation of practice, which are the unfailing fruits of authentic Christian allegiance always. Here is the justification for our dimly felt disquiet over the most militant Christian polemic of our time. And just here, I would suggest, should be the real crux of contemporary Christian controversy—not, in the first instance, in men's conceptions of God, the issues of Theism; or their interpretation of Christ and "Last Things," Christology and Eschatology; but in their silence as to the effective power of faith here and now.[6]

2) If Dr. Robinson's need is our need, is not the reason likewise the same: "a relative neglect of the Holy Spirit"?

---

[4] Psalms 51:1, 10.
[5] Galatians 5:22-23.
[6] This was the revealing and decisive inadequacy of the much-criticized "First Report" of the Advisory Commission on the Theme of the Second Assembly of the World Council of Churches. As one critic pointed out, "In the entire document there is only one incidental reference to the Holy Spirit." (Clarence Tucker Craig in *Ecumenical Review*, January 1952, p. 165.) Is not this the true message of "Christian Hope" for which our generation longs?

In current Christian thought, there is wanting an adequate
and convincing apprehension and appropriation of the Holy
Spirit.

To be sure, that neglect can claim notable historic ante-
cedents. It places us in the company of Christians of the
earliest centuries of Christianity, after the first. Our foremost
historian of thought concerning the Holy Spirit in the early
centuries began his first study with the statement: "In the
earliest age of the Church, comparatively little attention was
paid to the doctrine of the Holy Spirit."[7] It is a commonplace
of the history of Christian thought that, long after the mind
of the Church had formed its convictions concerning Christ
and had embodied those convictions in creeds, it had nothing
definite to say about the Holy Spirit. And for the very good
reason that it had given comparatively little attention to the
subject.[8] This may be a comforting precedent for our neglect.
It is no adequate excuse.

Broadly speaking, that neglect continued through the
centuries and has persisted to this day.

Within Protestantism, it has been especially noticeable in
Churches and theologies of the Calvinist tradition despite
their proud claim to theological adequacy and orthodoxy.
Witness the omission in the "Westminster Confession of
Faith" of any section on the Holy Spirit. This omission was
tardily and somewhat hesitantly rectified by the Presbyterian
Church U. S. A. after decades of controversy through the
addition to the Confession, in 1902, of a new chapter on
"Of the Holy Spirit."[9] Even so ecumenical a theologian as
the late Dr. William Adams Brown in his admirably "catho-

[7] H. B. Swete, *On the Early History of the Doctrine of the Holy Spirit*, p. 5.
[8] See below, Part II, Chapter 4, pp. 71 ff.
[9] Cf. Lefferts A. Loetscher, *The Broadening Church*, pp. 85-87.

lic" *Christian Theology in Outline* found no room for the
Holy Spirit save in a subsidiary section under a sub-heading
in his treatment of "The Christian Life"; and all that Dr.
Brown thought it important to say about the Holy Spirit was
readily compressed within three pages.

Examine the card-index of any comprehensive theological
library and one cannot fail to be impressed, and depressed,
by the relatively small number of volumes devoted to the
Holy Spirit; the great bulk of these date from the last
century. Open almost any one of the more recent treatments
of the Holy Spirit and one discovers its first page bemoaning
the neglect of the Holy Spirit in historic or contemporary
Christian theology or both with an almost monotonous same-
ness. Thus, one of the earliest treatises of any importance on
the Holy Spirit in the present century begins its preface with
these words:

> "It is a frequent and well-founded complaint that the
> doctrine of the Holy Spirit has been strangely neglected
> by theologians. Our theological text-books, as a rule,
> pass over the subject with a few conventional pages."[10]

And the latest opens on an identical note:

> "It has become almost a convention that those who
> undertake to write about the Holy Spirit should begin
> by deploring the neglect of this doctrine in the thought
> and life of the Church today."[11]

Nor is this neglect, and recognition of it, limited to Protestant theologians. As far back as 1897, Pope Leo XIII

[10] T. Rees, *The Holy Spirit in Thought and Experience* (1914), New York:
Charles Scribner's Sons, p. vii.
[11] From *The Holy Spirit in Christian Theology* by George S. Hendry, copyright
1956 by W. L. Jenkins, The Westminster Press, p. 11. Used by permission.

"expressed his bitter regret that Christians have but a meager knowledge of the Holy Spirit. 'They often use His name in their exercises of piety, but their faith is surrounded with dense darkness'; and he charged all preachers and those who have charge of souls to regard it as a duty to teach their people 'more diligently and more richly' on what concerns the Holy Spirit, so that the lamentable 'ignorance of these great and fruitful mysteries may be completely banished'."[12]

On the other hand, the desire so fervently voiced by Leo XIII that this neglect should be speedily rectified finds a clear echo in the few worthy Protestant works on the subject. Thirty years ago, that remarkable company of Oxford scholars known as the "Cumnor Group" who, under the shepherding of Canon B. H. Streeter, jointly produced a shelf of notable symposia sensed the same need and, aspiring to meet it, prefaced their composite volume on *The Spirit* with quotations from Professor Josiah Royce of Harvard and Frederick Denison Maurice.[13] Royce had written:

"The traditional doctrine of the Holy Spirit, neglected by the early theologians of the Church, even when the creeds were still in the formative period of their existence, has remained until this day in the background of inquiry, both for the theologians and for the philosophers. A favorite target for hostile, although often inarticulate, criticism on the part of the opponents of tradition, and a frequent object of reverential, but confessedly problematical and often very vague, ex-

---

[12] Charles Gore, *The Holy Spirit and the Church* (1924), p. 1.
[13] B. H. Streeter et al., *The Spirit,* New York: The Macmillan Company, p. viii. Used by permission.

position on the part of the defenders of the faith,—the article of the creed regarding the Holy Spirit is, I believe, the one matter about which most who discuss the problem of Christianity have least to say in the way of definite theory. Yet, if I am right, this is, in many respects, the really distinctive and therefore the capital article of the Christian creed."[14]

Royce's historical analysis was not far wrong. The Holy Spirit has been the step-child of Christian theology. And Maurice, half a century earlier, had made bold to prophesy:

"I cannot but think that the reformation in our day, which I expect to be more deep and searching than that of the sixteenth century, will turn upon the Spirit's presence and life, as that did upon the Justification by the Son."[15]

Maurice's forecast still lacks fulfillment. Broadly speaking, the Holy Spirit is today, as it has been through the Christian centuries, the neglected step-child of Christian theology.

This "lacuna" in the writing of the theologians has its parallel in the thought as well as the experience of the typical lay-Christian.

Of all the beliefs of Christian Faith, the Holy Spirit (and its companion, the Trinity) is for him the most mysterious and the most mystifying. Mysterious not in the right and desirable sense that it serves to remind him of the majesty of God which forever eludes men's best efforts to grasp Him or the manifoldness of God's goodness which forever surpasses man's readiness to receive Him, and so to enlarge

[14] Josiah Royce, quoted in *The Spirit,* ed. by B. H. Streeter, p. viii.
[15] Frederick Denison Maurice, quoted in *The Spirit, ibid.*

and enrich the layman's best thoughts of God; but mysterious
in the perverse and undesirable sense that it baffles and confuses him in trying to think of God worthily. God the Father
Almighty, he senses dimly as Creator and Sustainer of the
Universe. Only the most childish and inexcusable human
arrogance—lack of perspective, of sense of humor—ever
persuades the layman to deny Him, however perplexed he
may be as to just how to think of God and His relations to
men. Jesus Christ, the layman sees clearly set forth on the
pages of the Gospels, however much he may be puzzled by
Christian theology's claims for Him. But who or what is the
Holy Spirit?

One is reminded of the deacon, more candid than most,
who, when asked by his minister to define his conception of
God, replied that to him God was a "vague, oblong blur."
Most lay folk, let us hope, would hardly so describe their
thought of God. But, if pressed to reveal the idea which forms
in their minds at mention of the Holy Spirit, they might in
all honesty have recourse to the deacon's phrase, "a vague,
oblong blur." The mystification of the lay mind is, of course,
aggravated by the use of the mis-translation "Holy Ghost."
Whatever else the Holy Spirit may be, they suppose, it must
be something "ghostly."

If the Apostle Paul's question to the Christians at Ephesus
—"Have you received the Holy Spirit since you believed?"
(Acts: 19:1-7)—were put to our lay folk, they would hardly
answer, "We have not so much as heard whether there be any
Holy Spirit." But if his query were pressed more explicitly,
"Have you *received* the Holy Spirit?", might they not be
embarrassed to make reply? The spontaneous response of
not a few conscientious laymen and laywomen to the title

of this book might well be: "God and Christ, yes. But why the Holy Spirit?"

3.

Small wonder that the layman is confused in this matter. The fact is the Christian Church has never been altogether clear and consistent as to what is meant by the Holy Spirit. This fuzziness and inconsistency root back in the Bible itself, as we shall note later. That vagueness and confusion persisted through the early centuries and have continued down to our own day.

Sometimes, the Holy Spirit is thought of as the activity of God everywhere—in Creation, in man, in Jesus Christ, in the Christian Church; it denotes the *omnipresence of the Divine influence*. But, sometimes, the Holy Spirit is thought of solely as the touch of the Divine upon each man's inmost soul—clearly distinguished from God the Father Almighty, Creator of heaven and earth, and from Jesus Christ, His Son, our Saviour; it is the very *principle of personal religion*.

Sometimes, the Holy Spirit is pictured as descending upon men from without—as at Pentecost, with tongues of fire: *the Transcendent God in action*. But, sometimes, as a still, small voice within—as with the Friends; *the Immanent God in residence*.

Sometimes, men speak of the Holy Spirit in the most general and universal terms as indwelling the heart of every man—the *point-of-contact between Christianity and non-Christian faiths*. But some interpreters maintain that Christians know nothing of the Holy Spirit apart from Jesus

Christ.[16] And one great section of Christendom claims the Holy Spirit as exclusively *Christ's gift to His Church,* the living continuation of His Being, found within the corporate fellowship of His followers, and there only.

This uncertainty and inconsistency as to the being and activity of the Holy Spirit is not wholly an evidence of the muddleheadedness of Christians. In no small measure, it is a testimony to the manysidedness of God. It has been said, a trifle irreverently, that the Holy Spirit is the "catchall" of Christian theology. The truth is: every aspect of the Divine Being and Activity which could not readily be accounted for in terms of God the Father and Creator, or of Jesus Christ the Saviour, has been assigned to the Holy Spirit. Thus, the Holy Spirit has guarded Christians' thought of God from too precise formulation and too definitive limitation. It was a shrewd and revered leader of the Church in our day who confessed that his difficulty with the Christian doctrine of the Trinity was not to believe that there are three aspects of the Divine Being, but to be sure that there are only three. The Holy Spirit has kept Christians' thought of God "open-ended" toward new discoveries springing from new experiences of God, in turn testimonies to new revelations of Himself by God. And yet, with all the initially confusing varieties of meanings attached to the single term "Spirit" within the world of religion, two are distinctive and well-nigh universal —*intimacy* and *potency.* Characteristically, the Divine Spirit is recognized as an influence proceeding from the Ultimate

[16] So Professor George S. Hendry of Princeton Seminary in the most recent and one of the most suggestive and provocative treatments of the subject: "[Within the New Testament], the Spirit is presented in a purely Christocentric reference. There is no reference in the New Testament to any work of the Spirit apart from Christ. The Spirit is, in an exclusive sense, the Spirit of Christ." *The Holy Spirit in Christian Theology,* p. 26.

Divine Being, but not identical with that Being, marked by
the bestowal of exceptional powers, and closely related to the
life of man. The "Spirit of God" testifies to the immediately
present activity of the Divine—God-near and God-mighty.
The "Spirit of God" or "Holy Spirit" is always God-at-hand,
and the "Spirit of God" or "Holy Spirit" is always God-at-
work.

If additional justification were needed for the attention
which we propose to focus upon the theme of this book, it
could be found in the importance which the Holy Spirit
holds in the most dynamic and challenging Christian movements beyond the confines of traditional "ecumenical"
Protestantism in our day, the movements which we tend to
identify, a trifle condescendingly if not disparagingly, by a
term of mighty and noble meaning in the history of Christianity, "the Sects." For, multiform and often contrasted as
these movements are, almost without exception they attribute
their claim upon their followers and their right to a place
within authentic Christianity to their "recovery of the living
presence and power of the Holy Spirit." Thus, they stand
within one of the great traditions of Christian Faith. They
represent a reappearance, in the circumstances of our time
and in response to its special characteristics and needs, of
that ancient tradition.

4.

The "neglect" of the Holy Spirit to which we are pointing
is lamentable not only because the Holy Spirit should be a
central and vital factor in the individual Christian's thought

and life; it is also of immense importance for *Christianity's relations with other religions,* the whole world of religion in general.

Indeed, the first fact to be noted about the Holy Spirit is that, contrary to Professor Royce's statement above, it is not a uniquely or even distinctively Christian belief. Its interest for the theologian springs in no small measure from the fact that a conception not without at least superficial similarity to the Christian idea of the Holy Spirit is to be discovered near the heart of almost every living religion. This is true of non-Christian belief at its most elemental and "primitive" level and, no less, of the non-Christian faiths in their most developed and exalted expressions. Dr. E. F. Scott has well said, in introducing his admirable study of the Spirit in the New Testament: "The idea of the Spirit may thus be regarded as the constant factor in religion—linking the most advanced speculation of our own day with the first awakening of the higher life in man." And for this very good reason: "It has so remained constant because it has corresponded always with a genuine experience."[17]

These facts—the general prevalence of the idea of "Spirit" and the humble ancestry of the idea—should neither surprise nor confound the Christian. When we come to trace the history of the conception of "Spirit" through the Bible, we shall be compelled to acknowledge that there is no sharp point of transition or line of demarcation between the earliest identification of "spirit" with crudely natural forces and Paul's consummate insight: "The Lord is the Spirit."[18] In other words, even within Biblical thought, the "Spirit" may

[17] E. F. Scott, *The Spirit in the New Testament,* London: Hodder & Stoughton, Ltd., p. 11.
[18] II Corinthians 3:17.

be recognized as a connecting thread between that which is most primitive and that which is most advanced, between nature-wonder and God-worship. By the same token, men's thought of the Holy Spirit is the most significant meeting-point of the religions of mankind; therefore, the most revealing and fruitful basis for comparison both between elemental and mature religion and between the several higher religions.

We have said that the distinctive characteristics of the idea of "Spirit" are *intimacy* and *potency*. These are well-nigh unfailing marks of "primitive man's" first apprehensions of the Divine. These, in turn, root back in an even more elemental recognition of a "supernormal, diffused, impersonal force" which, Principal Micklem reminds us, "has no necessary connection with the idea of 'spirits' or of God."[19] This "force" which is "diffused" has come to be known among anthropologists and students of comparative religion, according to the terminology prevalent among the Melanesians, as "mana." "Anything that exceeded the usual strength of men or the usual course of nature was deemed the effect of mana. This power, perfectly distinct from normal physical forces, worked both for good and evil."[20] In brief, it appears that religion takes its rise, initially and universally, in men's recognition of a reality which is both immediately present and supernormally powerful; intimacy and potency are its aboriginal characteristics. When that diffused force is believed to reside in objects or animals or beings which behave in quasi-personal fashion, they are assumed to be indwelt by "spirit."

We have no intention of slipping into the familiar fallacy

[19] Nathaniel Micklem, *Religion*, p. 16.
[20] *Ibid.*

of much recent interpretation of religion, the bane of anthropological preoccupation—accounting for high religion in terms of its earliest origins—a fallacy parallel to modern psychology's tendency to explain consummate human achievement by examining the behavior of infants, or even guinea-pigs and mice! On the other hand, it is salutary to vaunting human pride to be reminded that the sublime has had its genesis in the elemental, and that there has been no radical break in its ancestry. Especially does this recognition supply corrective to the wrong kind of claim of uniqueness for Christian Faith. This recognition, honest attention to the genealogy of "spirit" dictates. That is a first and fundamental service of the Holy Spirit to Christian understanding.

However, it is the presence of the idea of Holy Spirit, not in religion at its most primordial level but in its noblest manifestations, which is of major interest. Here, the well-nigh universal presence of the Holy Spirit in non-Christian faiths may bring initial surprise. A competent student summarizes the evidence in these words:

> "The later Stoics spoke of a *spiritus sacer*—God, the *anima mundi,* who was conceived as a materialistic fiery breath, the intelligent permeating containing principle of the cosmos, resident in man and observant of his good and evil deeds."

> "In Greek mystery-religions we meet with 'Holy Spirit', which comes from God into the initiate at the mysteries."

> "In Muhammedanism the Holy Spirit, probably under Jewish influence, was identified with the angel Gabriel."

"Zoroastrianism speaks of a *spenta Mainyu* ('Holy
Spirit'), which is variously represented: as a personal
emanation of the God-head, as a created being probably
above the rank of angels, and even as identical with the
Supreme Creator, Ahura Mazda. He possesses creative
powers, ethical qualities, and teaching offices which
closely resemble the Christian view."[21]

More arresting than these descriptions of ideas strikingly
similar to the Christian conception of the Holy Spirit among
philosophies and faiths which originated within the same
geographical and cultural world as did the Hebrew-Christian
religion—in some instances, kinsfolk of that religion—is
the discovery of similar beliefs in faiths of utterly unrelated
origins. And more impressive than any amount of reported
testimony from the past is first-hand observation of evidence
in our own day. A single illustration must suffice.

On the outskirts of the city of Hong Kong is located one
of the most remarkable Christian institutions in the world.
Its founder, the late Doctor Karl Ludvig Reichelt, was a
Scandinavian Lutheran missionary with nearly half a century
of Christian service among Buddhists.

On a promontory high up above green hillsides with mag-
nificent panoramic views along the river valley and out
between steep hills toward the open sea, stands this unique
community. In English, it bears the name "The Buddhist-
Christian Institute," but the Chinese title "Tao Fongshan"
represents the three words: "Truth—Wind (or Spirit)—
Hill." It is the Hill of the Spirit of Truth, or the Hill of
the Word of God. In effect, it is a retreat or study center

[21] R. Birch Hoyle, "Spirit (Holy), Spirit of God," in Hastings, *Encyc. of Rel.
and Ethics*, New York: Charles Scribner's Sons, Vol. XI, p. 784.

where Buddhists, especially Buddhist priests, who wish to know more about Christianity may come to live, to study, to reflect. After their period of retreat, they may return to their Buddhist vocations. Or, if they desire, they may be baptized and even prepared for the Christian ministry.

The buildings are all in graceful Chinese style, many of them adaptations of what one might expect at a Buddhist monastery. One dormitory houses preliminary inquirers; another those who have crossed the divide into Christian allegiance and are now definitely in training in Christian Faith. The lecture-hall has sides wide open toward the air—and view. At the heart of the cluster of buildings stands the chapel —an octagonal building focussing upon a simple altar in its center. Beneath the dome and above the altar hangs the Star of Bethlehem. Here and there is the insignia of the fellowship or Order—an open lotus-lily (Buddhist symbol of unfolding truth) above which is suspended a Cross.

The Christian teaching is based largely upon the Johannine rendering of Christian Faith. For it is the basic premise of the Buddhist-Christian Institute that these two noblest among the living religions of mankind have in common the conception of Spirit of Truth, or Logos, or Word of God;[22] and that the Buddhist recognition of the living and present Spirit of Truth may discover its rightful fulfillment in the Christian reality of the Holy Spirit.[23] Of this premise, the Institute's symbol is the perfect representation—the Buddhist open-lily reaching up toward the Cross of Christ.

Probably this is the most notable meeting-place of two great

[22] We shall have something to say later about the kinship between the "Logos" and the "Holy Spirit," and the enrichment which might have come to Christian theology if the "Logos" of the Johannine interpretation had been permanently linked to the Third rather than to the Second Person of the Christian Trinity. See below, Chapter 2, p. 49 and Chapter 4, pp. 73 f.

[23] See Karl Reichelt in *The Authority of the Faith*, pp. 83 ff.

religions anywhere in the world. Here Buddhism and Christianity are brought into sympathetic confrontation with each other. The bridge from the former to the latter may be readily crossed; and in fact it is not infrequently traversed.

In summary, those who cleave to the Scriptural conviction that God has not left Himself without witness, at any time or among any people, may find abundant confirmation of that belief in the awareness of His Spirit—however dim and however crude—in the consciousness of humanity virtually everywhere and always. Those who, further, hold to the declaration of the Madras World Missionary Conference that His yearning after all His children, and His desire to win from them an answering recognition "has not been without response"[24] may point, as vindication, to the conceptions of Holy Spirit within the higher non-Christian faiths.

5.

From even so cursory a glance at the testimony of non-Christian religions, both elemental and advanced, these preliminary conclusions may be recorded:

1. The idea of "Divine Spirit" or "Spirit of God" or "Holy Spirit" is well-nigh omnipresent throughout mankind.

2. "Holy Spirit" is thought of characteristically as an emanation or giving-forth from the Divine. It connotes an activity of God, though not identical with the Ultimate Reality.

3. "Holy Spirit" is an immanent activity of God, in both the cosmos and man.

4. "Holy Spirit" is especially and intimately related to the

[24] *The World Mission of the Church*, p. 20.

experience of men, both their creation and their redemption.

We repeat, with all the initially confusing variety of meanings attached to the single term, Divine Spirit, within the world of religion, two are distinctive and universal—*intimacy* and *potency*. The Holy Spirit testifies to the immediately present activity of the Divine—God-near and God-mighty. The "Spirit of God" or "Holy Spirit" is always God-at-hand, and the "Spirit of God" or "Holy Spirit" is always God-at-work.

However, it is the unfailing and intimate linkage with "human experience," this rootage of conception in "experience," which is both the most striking and the most significant feature of the Holy Spirit everywhere and always. As Dr. Scott says:

> "The belief in the Spirit has always sprung out of an experience. It has been strongest in times of religious awakening, when men have grown suddenly aware that the truths they had clung to half mechanically are the great realities.

> "Men accepted the world as they found it, and tried to adjust themselves to its orderly conditions; but they were made aware, ever and again, of a disturbing element with which they had to reckon. What it was they did not know, but they recognized it only as a mysterious force, interfering with the settled arrangements of the world. . . . They have felt themselves possessed with a quickening and uplifting power, which seemed to come directly out of a higher world.

> "In all ages it has only been at rare intervals that men were lifted above the customary level of their lives, and

became capable of great things, and . . . they have con-
strued the action of the Spirit by their own experience."[25]

This has been, no less, the special characteristic of the Holy
Spirit in the Hebraic-Christian tradition: it has arisen out
of experience, as a datum of experience. And so the ablest
exposition of the doctrine in our time is on sound ground in
taking the title, "The Christian Experience of the Holy
Spirit." Awareness of the Holy Spirit is, usually, in direct
ratio to spiritual reality and vitality. If the belief "has been
strongest in times of religious awakening, when men have
grown suddenly aware . . . of the great realities," the obverse
holds: absence of clear certainty of the Holy Spirit is a sign
of deficiency in awareness of the Living God. Indeed, we
may detect a parallel to what I have elsewhere ventured to
call "the logic of spiritual vitality," re-enacted again and
again in the pilgrimage of the Christian Church, whereby a
period of intense and creative religious renewal is unfailingly succeeded by an aftermath of gradually diminishing
spiritual vigor but increasing theological and organizational
rigidity, then by a time of comparative sterility—until revival bursts forth afresh, and the curve of descending life
and power is re-enacted.[26] So with respect to the regnancy
of the Holy Spirit in Christian conviction. Here, too, the
historical review which we are to undertake will reveal a
closely parallel "logic of vitality." Time and again, the Holy
Spirit has dropped from the center of attention because it
has been lost from the heart of experience; theological
crystallization and controversy have preoccupied men's

[25] Scott, *op. cit.*, pp. vi, 13, vi, 19.
[26] See *World Christianity: Yesterday, Today and Tomorrow*, pp. 239-246.

minds; reliance upon creed and cult, upon form and structure, has displaced expectation of new disclosures, sometimes with determinative influence and often with baneful
effect upon men's conception of the Holy Spirit. Always,
perhaps at long last, the Holy Spirit has returned, first as an
experience and secondarily as a doctrine, to revive men's souls
and banish their defeat and despair, and then to reanimate
the dead skeletons of ecclesiastical organization and redeem
the dry rot of dogma.

A Church devoid of a vital and vibrant possession by the
Holy Spirit is a Church congealed in ancient forms, or well
on the way to spiritual sterility. Perhaps, here is the much-
discussed "lack" in the Church's life in our day. The "lacuna"
in Dr. Wheeler Robinson's understanding of evangelical
truth is, also, the decisive "lacuna" in the contemporary
Church's faith.

In this book we shall be principally concerned with the
place of the Holy Spirit in Christian theology, and especially
its significance for the other great beliefs of Christian Faith
—how Christians are to think about God and man and
Christ and the Church. But there should never be absent
from our minds the realization that the Holy Spirit is, first
and last, a reality of personal Christian apprehension, of
utmost consequence for the most urgent needs of each one
of us.

6.

Against this very general and introductory background, we
turn, in our next three chapters, to a summary survey of the
presence and development of recognition of the Holy Spirit

within the Hebrew-Christian tradition of which we are heirs—to the "Biography of a Great Conviction." But both perspective and added value will be furnished to our study if we recall that it is directed toward something more than a merely Christian reality, to one of the universal and clamant concerns of mankind.

Moreover, our interest in the history is by no means antiquarian or pedantic. On the contrary, men's understanding, and misunderstandings, of the Holy Spirit in the past have surprisingly close parallels to both the promise and the perplexities in our comprehension of its meaning for us today. This relevance, we shall attempt to discover at every point.

THE
BIOGRAPHY
OF A
GREAT
CONVICTION

The Bible has been called, with pardonable exaggeration, "The Book of the Spirit."[1]

Its first page portrays the Spirit of God "brooding, like a mother bird, upon the face of the waters," bringing order and beauty and meaning out of primordial chaos.[2] Its last page cries forth the Spirit's glorious invitation: "The Spirit and the bride say 'Come' . . . And let him that is athirst come. And whosoever will, let him take the water of life freely."[3] From the birth of Nature at creation to the rebirth of man's soul to eternal life, the Bible records the ceaseless activity of the Spirit.

Statistics may seem an external and uncertain guide to spiritual significance. But it is a rough and ready calculus to the prevalence of the activity of "spirit" throughout Scripture that in the Old Testament "spirit" occurs no fewer than 378 times, and in the New Testament 335 times. The simple device of taking one's Bible and underscoring with a red pencil each appearance of the word will reveal the pages, especially and most significantly those of the New Testament, dotted with red.

[1] H. Wheeler Robinson, *The Christian Experience of the Holy Spirit*, p. 5.
[2] Genesis 1:2.
[3] Revelation 22:17.

CHAPTER TWO

THE OLD TESTAMENT

Is it possible to discover any major line or lines of development in Hebraic thought about the Spirit of God, from the earliest period to the eve of the New Testament?

Acknowledging the hazards to such generalization, because of the many diverse strands which have become inwoven like a patternless fabric to form our texts and the uncertainty of their respective dates, and recognizing the tentative character of our conclusions, it is possible to discern roughly *five stages* in the pilgrimage (not, in each instance, progress, however) of the dominant Hebrew recognition of the Spirit of God.

1.

The chronicle begins, as we should expect, in the dim hinterland of pre-history and on the border-line between the thought of the Hebrews and that of other peoples of the same epoch or at a similar stage of development. The level is not far above that of primitive animism.

35

As is well known, the Hebrew word "ruäḥ" signifies, in the first instance, "air-in-motion," either wind or breath— the mighty, mysterious and scorching wind of the desert, the pervasive atmosphere which seems to sustain Nature, *or* the gentle, no less mysterious, animating breath which indwells the living body, the secret of its vitality without which it ceases to exist. And so a secondary meaning of "ruäḥ" is power-in-manifestation or energy, whether in the cosmos or in animate creation.

Extraordinary phenomena of all kinds, both in physical Nature and in animate Nature, especially those marked by manifestations of unusual power, are attributed to the operation of Spirit.

Indeed, of the 378 uses of the single word in the Old Testament, almost a third (131) describe merely *physical* phenomena, air-in-motion, the wind. Another 39 occurrences have a *physiological* reference, to the breath of animals and men, air-in-motion in the body, the principle of life. In another 74 instances, "ruäḥ" carries a *psychical* connotation; it is the emotional or mental aspects of the experience of human beings which is indicated—anger, grief, fear, etc. The realistic and naturalistic cast of the Hebrew mind is clearly revealed in the transition from the first to the second, and from the second to the third range of meanings. Breath is the most obvious evidence of life; in sickness or fainting, the breath falters, suggesting that the "spirit" or vehicle of life is impaired; at death, breathing ceases, and the "spirit" has left the body altogether. Thus it was that the Lord God "breathed into man's nostrils the breath of life, and man became a living soul";[4] and, at death, "the spirit shall return

4 Genesis 2:7.

unto God who gave it."[5] Again, under strong emotion, whether fear or anger or jealousy or grief, breathing is disturbed and accentuated; therefore, thought the Hebrews, a "spirit" of the particular emotion has entered the person and "possesses" him. Finally, by another natural transition, 134 times in the Old Testament "Spirit" carries a *supernatural* meaning, to mark agencies operating upon man from without and from beyond Nature. Initially, these "spirits" might be of evil no less than of good; then, though still evil as well as good, they were all conceived as under the control and direction of God; ultimately, "spirit" is reserved to its Divine source as "the spirit of God."

To this earliest period belong the familiar incidents of the visitations of the Spirit upon Gideon and Samson and Saul and David and Elijah.

"The Spirit of the Lord took possession of Gideon." (Judges 6:34)

"The woman bore a son, and called his name Samson. . . . and the Spirit of the Lord began to stir him. . . . And the Spirit of the Lord came mightily upon him." (Judges 13:24-25; 14:6)

"The Spirit of the Lord came mightily upon him [Saul]." ". . . The Spirit of the Lord departed from Saul." (I Samuel 10:10; 16:14)

"These are the last words of David. . . . 'The Spirit of the Lord speaks by me.' " (II Samuel 23:1-2)

[5] Ecclesiastes 12:7. Cp. Luke 8:55 where, when Jesus revives the seemingly dead girl, it is explained, "Her spirit came again."

"And Elisha said [to Elijah], 'I pray you, let me inherit a double share of your spirit.'" (II Kings 2:9)

In these most primitive manifestations of "spirit," its marks are supernormal energy or extraordinary behavior, not infrequently ecstasy or frenzy and inarticulate and meaningless utterance. As just mentioned, the effect of the influence of Spirit may be, ethically regarded, either good or evil. "In the earlier literature the Spirit has nothing to do with ethical ideas. It is simply the power whereby a man is made capable of marvellous action, without any regard to the moral value of what he does."[6]

Indeed, it is important to recognize to the full the non-moral and even sub-moral characteristics of many of these earliest attributions to the work of the Spirit. Our major interest is the discovery and recovery of the loftiest truths within the authentic Christian apprehension of the Holy Spirit. But we need constantly to be reminded of its humble origins and associations, in order that we may identify the sub-Christian elements in its ancestry which, like an inherited infection descending unto the third and fourth, yes unto the thirtieth and fortieth generations, are forever reappearing and laying claim to be of the true character of the Holy Spirit. Here, for example, we meet the early anticipation of some of the cruder "signs of the Spirit" in Early Christianity, both "spirit-possession" and demon-possession, and "speaking with tongues." No less, however, of Pentecostal spirit-possession in our own day, just as the primitive assumption that eating the flesh of a "spirit-possessed" animal or even human being would transmit to the eater supernormal energy or

[6] Scott, *The Spirit in the New Testament*, p. 15.

power anticipates realistic claims to the impartation of "spirit" through partaking of the elements in the Christian sacrament. Here is a first warning to us—of the unruly and extravagant manifestations attributed to the Spirit—throughout Biblical times, and right on down to our own day.

Varied as are the manifestations of the Divine Spirit, crudely animistic and non-moral as they often are, all references to the Spirit of God appear to be held in unity at one point: "The Spirit of God is God at work manifesting effective power."[7] Intimacy and potency are its unfailing marks. So humble and earthy, and so elemental and essential, is the direct ancestry of the Christian idea of the Holy Spirit.

2.

The second stage of the pilgrimage is marked by an internal struggle within the soul of Hebrew faith between these primordial and amoral strains in thought of the Spirit and the ethical consciousness of the early prophets, striving to establish their loftier understanding of Jahweh. To say the same thing in other words, God as righteous Sovereign battles, in the mind of the faith, to subdue the unworthy elements previously assigned to His Spirit. It is noteworthy that the earlier prophets eschew any claim to possession by or even authorization by the Spirit. Amos and Hosea, Micah and Isaiah and Jeremiah, all derive their authority directly from God: "The Lord said unto me." "Thus saith the Lord."

[7] R. Birch Hoyle, "Spirit (Holy), Spirit of God," in *H.E.R.E.*, Vol. XI, p. 786. Cp. A. B. Davidson on Ezekiel 36:27, quoted in H. B. Swete, "Holy Spirit," in Hastings, *Dict. of Bible,* Vol. II, p. 404: "The Spirit of God is God exerting power."

Hosea's single reference declares the prevailing view that "He that hath the Spirit is mad." (9:7) The solitary reference in Micah (3:8) suffers from textual uncertainty. Jeremiah disregards the Spirit altogether. Almost certainly, this silence is due to the discredit of the Spirit among men of highest ethical sensitivity because of its customary association with abnormal and fantastic behavior.

Here, likewise, is warning for us, especially when we discover later a similar reticence about the Spirit on the part of Him who is greater than all the prophets.[8] For here, again, is anticipation of later and more familiar struggles—Paul against the crude claims to "spirit-possession" by Christians in Corinth and elsewhere; the revolt of the Reformers against a medieval mysticism centered in an "Urgrund" which was "beyond good and evil"; the habitual opposition of all traditionalisms to fresh outpourings of "the Spirit" because of their excesses and aberrations; even the suspicion which attaches to the Friends' "guidance of the Holy Spirit" when it is described in non-personal, and therefore, sub-moral terms. Authentic awareness of the "power of the Spirit" must always tussle against the fascination of the merely spectacular and the demoralization of crude potency.

But the right resolution of the battle is never excommunication of the Spirit. Prophetic history anticipated Paul's solution no less than Paul's problem. The conviction of the Spirit sprang too powerfully from genuine experience and accorded too closely to Reality to suffer banishment. The final upshot of the prophets' struggle was not denial of the Spirit but its moralization into conformity with their highest vision of God. The later Isaiah and Ezekiel reclaim the inspiration of the Spirit. "The Spirit is now in a real and

---

[8] See below, Chapter 3, pp. 53 ff.

intimate sense the Spirit of the Lord. Its one function is to accomplish the will of God, and its attributes are all understood in the light of the divine character . . . The prophets often speak indifferently of 'God' and 'the Spirit of God.' "[9] Henceforward, the route of the Spirit's pilgrimage is largely parallel to, indeed controlled by, developments in the Hebrew thought of God Himself.

3.

The next stage was determined by the intense preoccupation of the Hebrew mind with the relation of the Nation to Jahweh. As religion became more nationalistic, so did the prevailing interpretation of the Spirit. For a time, it is thought of as the peculiar possession of Israel. Again, an anticipation of an issue which was much later to become central in Christian theology inescapably suggests itself. The Divine Spirit did not have to wait until the fully articulated doctrine of the Church, or even until the days of Early Christianity, to suffer imprisonment within the exclusive claims of some particular self-designated corporate repository of special Divine favor. Here once more, is a pointed warning to us.

4.

But neither the Hebrew thought of God, nor of His Spirit, could be constrained permanently within man-conceived limitations and man-constructed captivity. As we should expect, the pilgrimage of the Old Testament under-

[9] Scott, *op. cit.,* p. 30.

standing of the Spirit climbs to its loftiest heights—though unfortunately, not its final destination—in the consciousness of the greatest prophets and their contemporaries among the psalmists and seers.

Three different points of view distinguish these consummatory comprehensions of the Spirit within the Old Testament. And they should be kept clearly distinguished in our minds. For while they may have been roughly contemporary, they are by no means mutually consistent. And, in our effort to lay hold of the highest thought, we shall be compelled to make judgment between them:

> a. With some writers, and they the most influential, the time perspective is radically altered from the present to the past and future. They speak, not of what the Spirit of God *is* doing, but of what He *has done* and it is hoped He *will do*. The actual functioning of the Spirit is no longer contemporary but retrospective or anticipatory.
>
> b. With some, a very few but they among the most profound, the Spirit's domain is again widened from human life, whether corporate or individual, to embrace the cosmos.
>
> c. With some of the writers, and they the noblest, the Spirit is no longer primarily a factor in national history, or in the cosmos, but rather a reality of most intimate individual experience. The personal reference triumphs over the corporate.

Let us examine these three types of interpretation in order:

a. As illustrations of the first we may cite Ezekiel and

Joel. Ezekiel, still preoccupied with the destiny of Israel as God's elect, rises to foretell the reanimation and redemption of the nation: "A new heart also will I give you, and a new spirit will I put within you. . . . And I will put my Spirit within you, and cause you to walk in my statutes, and ye shall keep my judgments, and do them." (36:26-27) Joel carries the promise of Divine blessing a step farther to envision the renewal of humanity, and of all ranks and classes of mankind: "I will pour out my Spirit upon all flesh; and your sons and your daughters shall prophesy, your old men shall dream dreams, your young men shall see visions: and also upon the servants and upon the handmaids in those days will I pour out my Spirit." (2:28-29) Here, we discern a measure of fusion of the first with the third characteristics; the gift of the Spirit is to come to individuals, and to individuals of all stations. But, for both Ezekiel and Joel, the visitation of the Spirit is not present but future. In both respects, they point the way to those even more exalted forecasts which Christian interpretation has traditionally regarded as the climax of the Old Testament pilgrimage and the bridge across which the faith passed to its fulfillment in Christ—*the anticipation of the Messiah:*

> "The Spirit of the Lord shall rest upon him, the spirit of wisdom and understanding, the spirit of counsel and might, the spirit of knowledge and of the fear of the Lord . . . for the earth shall be full of the knowledge of the Lord, as the waters cover the sea." (Isaiah 11:2, 9)

> "Behold my servant, whom I uphold; mine elect, in whom my soul delighteth; I have put my Spirit upon him. . . . He shall not fail nor be discouraged, till he

have set judgment in the earth: and the isles shall wait
for his law." (Isaiah 42:1, 4)

And, especially, *the response of the Servant of the Lord*—
the passage which many Christians cherish most within the
whole range of the Old Testament as anticipatory of the
New:

> "The Spirit of the Lord God is upon me; because the
> Lord hath anointed me . . . to proclaim the acceptable
> year of the Lord." (Isaiah 61:1, 2)

b. The Hebrew mind, notoriously concrete and "existen-
tial" rather than abstract and metaphysical, troubled itself
but little with speculations regarding the origin and destiny
of the cosmos, which loomed so prominently in Greek,
Oriental and Egyptian thought of the same epoch. But Job,
in his soul's agony, cries that "By his Spirit God hath gar-
nished the heavens." (Job 26:13) And the author of
Ecclesiastes and an occasional psalmist echo a similar conviction.

We must turn to the opening page of Genesis, however, to
find a comprehensive treatment of the mystery of Creation.
For the words which stand first in our Old Testament voice
among its latest and most mature thoughts. And there we
are told that that Spirit of God which, much earlier, had
been pictured as "breathing into man's nostrils the breath of
life, so that man became a living soul" (Genesis 2:7), had
also "moved upon the face of the waters" (Genesis 1:2) to
bring into being the cosmos itself. Both creation stories, so
widely separated in age of composition and no less in level
of spiritual discernment, are implicitly universal in their

teaching. The Spirit of God which formed the world is also the Bestower of life upon all men.

Thus, a conception is spelled forth which prepares the way for the recognition of that same Spirit of God, now known as altogether Righteous and Holy, as a Living Presence of truth and mercy and power, intimately available to every eager and humble soul; yes, an inescapable Presence.

c. For the fulfillment of this promise—the noblest expression of the third of the interpretations which we have distinguished—we must turn, not to the prophets, even the greatest of them, but to the psalmists. And to two psalms in particular. Here, rather than in even the treasured visions of Messianic forecast, some would hold (and frankness compels me to confess myself among them), is to be found the mountain-summit of pre-Christian faith:

> "O Lord, thou hast searched me, and known me.
> "Thou hast beset me behind and before, and laid thine hand upon me.
> "Whither shall I go from thy Spirit? or whither shall I flee from Thy presence?" (Psalm 139:1, 5, 7)

The omnipresence ("Everywhere-ness") of the Spirit of God! Here, the early marks of the Spirit—intimacy and potency—and the later characteristics—righteousness and compassion—are knit into one mighty conception. And that Spirit is no reminiscence of a bygone past and no hoped-for incursion into some later age, but the most certain and immediately and always near Presence—"closer than breathing, nearer than hands and feet." To that understanding of the Spirit of God, there is only one appropriate response of the honest and contrite heart:

> "Search me, O God, and know my heart: try me, and know my thoughts: and see if there be any wicked way in me, and lead me in the way everlasting." (Psalm 139:23-24)

In the same vein speaks "the Psalm of the Spirit" which is, in the estimate of many, the noblest utterance of the whole Old Testament:

> "Have mercy upon me, O God, according to thy loving-kindness: according unto the multitude of thy tender mercies blot out my transgressions. . . .
> "Create in me a clean heart, O God; and renew a right spirit within me. Cast me not away from thy presence; and take not thy Holy Spirit from me.
> "Restore unto me the joy of thy salvation; and uphold me with thy free Spirit." (Psalm 51:1, 10-12)

Added meaning rises from the fact that only in this psalm and once elsewhere in the Old Testament (Isaiah 63:10, 11) is the Spirit denominated "holy." Here, likewise, is no fevered or visionary anticipation of future visitation, but quiet, assured declaration of present transformation. And the mood induced by that certainty is not hope for some undated deliverance, but gratitude, penitence and dedication prompted by experienced redemption.

I have made bold to stress the contrast between these three different strands of high Old Testament thought because I do not see how that contrast can be denied, or the respective faiths fully reconciled. Once again, we confront in anticipation a crucial issue for the understanding and interpretation of the Holy Spirit in every subsequent age: Is the Holy Spirit a promise of a coming Divine Deed which shall displace the existing order of experience; or is the Holy Spirit God's present gift to the humble and yearning heart, indwelling it and transforming it here and now into the image of His beauty and grace? The issue may be made concrete in this troubling question which we would prefer not to ask: Which do you consider the noblest interpretation of the Spirit prior to the Advent of Christ—the visions of Ezekiel and Joel and the Second Isaiah *or* the assurance of the 139th and 51st Psalms? The contrast, and its inescapable question, become more pointed as we turn to the next and final stage of the Spirit's pilgrimage through the Old Testament.

5.

The passages we have just cited mark the loftiest summit of Old Testament thought regarding the Spirit. Unhappily, they do not mark the end. There is an aftermath, which is anticlimax. For between the great prophets, the greater seer of Genesis 1 and the even greater psalmists, and the New Testament writers intervene several centuries of later Judaism, reflected in the last additions to the Old Testament and in the Apocrypha. With respect to thought of the Spirit, two facts stand forth.

On the one hand, so far as the Spirit is referred to at all, the tendency to conceive its operation as deferred to the future and in terms of radical incursion into the normal course of history is aggravated in both respects. The noble eschatology of Ezekiel and Joel and the Second Isaiah gives place to the extravagant apocalypticism of the Book of Enoch.

The more striking fact, however, is the virtual disappearance of the Spirit as an active and present factor in faith. The Spirit is a voice which formerly spoke by the prophets or a Supernatural Agent who will some day come again in a future Deliverer. What a far cry from the Creator of Genesis and the Redeemer of Psalms 139 and 51! The basic reason is not far to seek. "Belief in the Spirit had its ground in certain experiences, and in the religion of the later age these had become unusual, and to a great extent unreal . . . They look forward to a future age in which the Spirit will again be active, but are conscious that for the present it has been withdrawn."[10] However, Hebrew faith, thus deprived of its most enriching present possession, did not remain empty. Elaborate angelologies replaced the Holy Spirit of the Living God. Ecclesiasticism articulated itself in cult and priesthood and dogma. And Hebrew thought, thus bereft of its most challenging and quickening conviction, did not remain idle. To a very considerable extent, meditation on the Spirit was displaced by speculations influenced in no small measure by alien philosophies emanating from Alexandria and elsewhere—Hellenism, Stoicism, Philo. Here, once more, are anticipations of developments in the thought of the Faith in later ages when, again, awareness of the Living and Potent Spirit of God as an immediately present Reality has grown dim.

Implicit in this turning toward speculation and toward foreign systems of thought was one possibility which, had

[10] Scott, *op. cit.,* pp. 47, 50. However, the Dead Sea Scrolls have disclosed a vivid awareness of the Spirit among the Essenes and doubtless other sect groups of the period.

it seen realization, might have worked decisive modification of Hebraic-Christian thought concerning the Spirit, for good or for ill, and perhaps for all time. Within that surrounding thought-world, there was a single conception which was well-nigh universal, present alike in Platonism, Stoicism and the more popular cults. It was the idea of the Logos. Its natural affinity, in many of its expressions, with the Old Testament thought of the Spirit is obvious. But, strangely, though the idea of the Logos was married in this period to one of the ruling Hebrew ideas, it was not that of the Spirit but rather that of Wisdom. The reasons are interesting occasions for guesswork. Possibly because Wisdom was a more speculative and cosmic category, more readily mated with the Hellenistic Logos. Possibly because the marriage was arranged in Alexandria where Wisdom was more highly regarded. Perhaps, again, because the Spirit had, for the time, ceased to be a sufficiently living reality to warrant serious consideration. Whatever the reason, the fact is indisputable and of immense import. We can well defer consideration of it until we come to a closely parallel query in the post-New Testament period: What would have been the consequences for Christian theology if the Logos had been identified with the Third rather than the Second Person in the Christian triune conception of God, with the Spirit rather than with Christ?

6.

In summary, in the thought of the Hebrew people, of which our Christian Faith is the child and with which it is directly continuous, as Hebraic thought is disclosed to us in the Scriptures of our Old Testament, "spirit" holds a large and important place. It is initially a term of very wide and inclusive reference; it identifies the principle of life in both Nature and man. Always, it carries a two-fold meaning: it signifies vitality or activity, and it signifies intimacy or immediacy.

As the Hebrew mind advanced in its understanding of both man and God, so likewise did its comprehension of "spirit."

There is much evidence, not that men rose from the crude idea of breath as the life-giving principle in themselves to that of spirit, and then read that conception of spirit into their thought of God; but, rather, that they came to understand the nature of God no longer as "wind" or "breath" but as Spirit, and then dared to interpret their own natures as likewise spirit. Of this meaning of Spirit, also, the New Testament bears witness supremely—"The Spirit itself beareth witness with our spirit, that we are the children of God: And, if children, then heirs; heirs of God, and joint-heirs with Christ." (Romans 8:16-17)

More particularly, the age-long struggle to achieve a more worthy conception of Deity is perfectly mirrored in the slow and painful development of the idea of Divine Spirit, from suggestions of crude potency to recognition of righteous and holy might, from exclusive association with a "Chosen People" to presence among all peoples, from stress upon extraordinary manifestations in Nature to emphasis upon omnipresence throughout Creation but especially within the souls of persons.

It reaches fulfillment in the conviction that the Divine Spirit as God's agent in creation has bestowed his very self upon each human being, thus made in the Divine image; and that that same Divine Spirit continues to encompass each human spirit, watching over its every outward act and inmost aspiration, forever reclaiming it with pardon and with power to its true destiny as veritably the child of the Divine Father.

But, just as the Hebrew soul was under necessity to liberate its thought of spirit in God and man from crude and unworthy associations, so it had to struggle to maintain its loftiest understandings against the ever-present drag of the primitive and the superstitious, the merely marvellous and miraculous; and, in a time when certitude of the living empowerment of the Divine Spirit had grown dim, it yielded to the all-too-natural temptation to assume that that Spirit had been withdrawn from the affairs of men but would return in catastrophic intervention at some undated future. It was amidst such eclipse of the higher faith that Christianity was born.

CHAPTER THREE

THE NEW TESTAMENT

If the Bible has been called, with some exaggeration, "the Book of the Spirit," we may more readily accept Dr. Birch Hoyle's dictum that "The New Testament is pre-eminently the book of the Holy Spirit. Every writing except the Second and Third Letters of John refers to it; each Gospel opens with the promise of its effusion; the Acts is devoted to its operation in the creation, guidance and expression of the Christian Church; whilst the Epistles constantly refer to its working in the individual and collective life of believers."[1]

The vocabulary of the New Testament is not uniform in referring to the Spirit. Of the more than three hundred (335) uses, over half (220) speak simply of "Spirit" or "the Spirit," while the term "Holy Spirit" which had occurred only twice in the Old Testament appears ninety-one times, "The Spirit of God" or "the Spirit of the Lord" or "the Spirit of the Father" nineteen times, and "the Spirit of Christ" five times. The relation between these variant terms furnishes one of the most interesting and suggestive themes for inquiry; in-

[1] R. Birch Hoyle, "Spirit (Holy), Spirit of God," in *H.E.R.E.*, Vol. XI, p. 791.

deed, if we are not mistaken, it is precisely in a right understanding of that relationship that the secret of a true comprehension of the Holy Spirit lies.

I. THE SYNOPTIC GOSPELS

When we pass from the pages of the Old Testament to
those of the New and make our beginning (as our New
Testament does and as we should always do) with the Gospels of Matthew, Mark, and Luke, we are at once confronted
by an arresting, an astounding contrast:

> In the spoken words of Jesus as recorded in the first
> three Gospels, the "Spirit" or "Holy Spirit" hardly
> occurs upon his lips.

> With the major events of Jesus' life as reported by these
> same Gospels, the Holy Spirit is almost always vitally
> connected, not infrequently as their determinative
> cause.

This contrast is further heightened, and complicated, by
the fact that, in the Gospel of John, unlike the Synoptics,
Jesus is repeatedly recorded as referring to the Holy Spirit.

Earlier, I suggested that, if one wished to gain a graphic
impression of the prevalence of the Spirit throughout the
Bible, he might have recourse to the homely device of underlining references to it in red pencil. But if one were to take
a "red letter New Testament" in which the words of Jesus
are printed in red and continue underlining in red references

to the Spirit, he could not but be struck by the paucity of red marks beneath the red type.

Actually, in the total record of Jesus' utterances as transmitted by the Synoptists, the word "Holy Spirit" or its equivalent appears just five times:

> 1. One reference occurs only in Luke: "How much more will your Heavenly Father give the Holy Spirit to those who ask Him." (Luke 11:13) But the parallel passage in Matthew (7:11) reads "give good gifts." In view of Luke's special interest in the Holy Spirit, Matthew's version may be accepted as more accurate.

> 2. There is a similar divergence between Matthew's quotation, "If I by the Spirit of God cast out demons" (12:28), and Luke's rendering, "If I with the finger of God" (11:20); but, in this instance, recognizing Luke's partiality to the Holy Spirit, it is probable that his rather than Matthew's version is authentic.

> 3. A third allusion is to the Old Testament, the source of David's inspiration—"For David himself said by the Holy Spirit." (Mark 12:36 and Matthew 22:43) This instance may, perhaps not unfairly, be dismissed with the recognition that Jesus here merely follows the customary explanation of Divine inspiration; though, as with His habitual acceptance of the prevailing interpretation of the influence of "evil spirits" upon people's lives, it is interesting to note that Jesus attempts no revision of popular usage.

> 4. A much more interesting and important reference to the Holy Spirit, appearing in all three Gospels as

parallels, occurs in Jesus' reported instructions to his followers in the face of opposition: "It is not you who speak, but the Holy Spirit." (Mark 13:11; Matthew 10:20; Luke 12:12) However, presumably Mark is the original source for both Matthew and Luke; in Mark, these words appear in a section of the Gospel whose reliability is widely doubted; in any event, the whole setting of the instructions suggests circumstances of the Early Church rather than of the Life of Jesus.

5. Lastly, there is an instance, also in all three Gospels, which comes early in the record and which competent New Testament scholars are disposed to regard as of most probable authenticity: "He that shall blaspheme against the Holy Spirit shall never be forgiven." (Mark 3:29; Matthew 12:31; Luke 12:10)

In summary, the authors of the first three Gospels, in the whole of their account of Jesus' comment and teaching, mention five occasions when he referred to the Holy Spirit. Two of these must be summarily dismissed on the basis of comparison with obviously more reliable parallels in other Gospels. One merely echoes popular usage. Another is highly dubious in the eyes of critical scholarship. This leaves just one saying for which strong claims of authenticity can be lodged: "He that shall blaspheme against the Holy Spirit shall never be forgiven." It is Dr. Ernest Scott's considered judgment: "This would appear to be the only incontestible reference to the Spirit in the Synoptic teaching; Jesus declares that the power behind his miracles is that of the Spirit."[2]

[2] Scott, *The Spirit in the New Testament*, p. 76. Dr. Scott reviews this whole matter thoroughly.

When we turn from the reported utterances of Jesus to the narrative of His life, we meet the activity of the Holy Spirit at almost every crucial point:

> According to Luke, his coming was preceded by a widespread outpouring of the Holy Spirit—upon Elizabeth and Zacharias and Simeon. (Luke 1:41, 67; 2:25)

> In the independent though closely parallel accounts of Jesus' conception in Matthew and Luke, the Holy Spirit comes upon Mary. (Matthew 1:18; Luke 1:35)

> The boy Jesus grows and waxes strong in spirit. (Luke 1:80; 2:40)

> At his baptism at the hands of John, the Holy Spirit descends upon him. (Matthew 3:16; Mark 1:10; Luke 3:22. Cp. John 1:29-34)

> Immediately thereafter, he is led forth by the Spirit into the wilderness to wrestle with temptations to an unworthy fulfillment of his vocation. (Matthew 4:1; Mark 1:12; Luke 4:1)

> He returns from his testing in the wilderness "in the power of the Spirit" to enter upon his life's work. (Luke 4:14)

> At his first public appearance, in the synagogue of his home town of Nazareth, he announces his mission in revered and stirring words of Isaiah's forecast, "The Spirit of the Lord is upon me," and declares that "This day is this Scripture fulfilled." (Luke 4:16-21)

Lastly, after his death has been succeeded by resurrec-
tion, he appears to give final directions to those who
are to continue his work in words which close the
Synoptic record: "Baptize in the name of the Father,
and of the Son, and of the Holy Spirit." (Matthew
28:19)

Moreover, throughout his ministry, he exorcises evil
spirits (e.g., Mark 5:8; 9:25; Matthew 12:43; also Mark
1:23-27; 6:7; Matthew 8:16; Luke 7:21; 8:2; 9:42); but
never by invoking the power of the Holy Spirit.

As suggested above, the contrast to which we have been
calling attention is further heightened, and complicated, by
the fact that, in the Gospel of John, unlike the Synoptics,
Jesus is repeatedly recorded as referring to the Holy Spirit.
This double contrast would stand forth unresolved, utterly
mystifying and inexplicable, were it not for a further fact
which supplies the background for our accounts of both
words and events, the enveloping atmosphere in which both
were set down: the life of the Early Church in which the
memories of words and events were preserved and ultimately
recorded was permeated, indeed dominated, by the presence
and direction of the Holy Spirit.

2. THE EARLIEST CHURCH

In the chronicles of the Earliest Church in the Book of
Acts, the records which stand next in date of original formulation (though not in final arrangement) to the reported
words of Jesus in the Synoptic Gospels, the Holy Spirit ap-

pears on virtually every page. If enthusiasts may be accused
of exaggeration in calling the Bible "the Book of the Spirit"
or the New Testament "the Book of the Holy Spirit," no
one will challenge the statement that Acts is pre-eminently
and above everything "the Chronicle of the Holy Spirit's
activity." This is the connecting thread which weaves its
way ceaselessly in and out of the accounts of the many and
diverse events.

It is often said that in Early Christianity as portrayed in
Acts, the Holy Spirit is primarily an agent of the Church.
Such a generalization seems to me a gravely faulty reading
of the evidence. To be sure, its first appearance is to the
assemblage of disciples "in the Upper Room" on the Day
of Pentecost (2:1-4), and from that moment the Christian
Church was born; the Holy Spirit *is* the creator of the Church
but *not* its creature. And the gift of the Christian Holy
Spirit comes, necessarily, only to those within the Christian
fellowship. Dr. Scott is closer to the facts when he affirms:
"The sphere in which it works is always the Christian
Church. . . . The Spirit is the gift of Christ to his people,
and no one outside of their fellowship can share in it. . . .
As the gift of Christ to his people the Spirit, for New Testament thought, has its sphere of action in the Christian
Church."[3] Thus, the way is prepared for one aspect of the
final phase of Paul's thought about the Spirit in which it
becomes the very principle of the Church's being.

But even these more careful statements might convey a
distorted impression. Actually, the Spirit comes most characteristically to individuals, often when outside the immediate
fellowship of the Church, and sometimes with directives
defiant of the convictions and instructions of the Church.

[3] Scott, *ibid.,* pp. 88, 89, 120.

(e.g., Acts 11:12) The unfailing mark of its advent was augmentation of power. It found expression in glossolalia, speaking with tongues, ecstasy, prophecy, miraculous healings, and kindred extraordinary and extranormal happenings. Thus, it stood in the lineage of some of the more primitive strands in the ancestry of the Spirit. But the Holy Spirit also brought supernormal courage, insight, skill in argument, even business acumen. In other words, the fruit of the Spirit was the heightening of all the normal powers—intellectual, physical and spiritual—and their effective employment in the service of the Church. However, its most notable gift, and the one which most merits careful study in the search for a full and true understanding of the Holy Spirit, was direction or command—"the guidance of the Holy Spirit." The Holy Spirit is the donor of direct and immediate instruction from God, and that leading is toward the new, the unexpected, the mandatory. Of this, the forecast attributed to Jesus by the Fourth Gospel was the promise: "The Counselor, the Holy Spirit, whom the Father will send in my name, he will teach you all things." (John 14:26) Or, more accurately, this "forecast" was a backward reflection of the experienced realization of the Church in the time of John's writing. The Holy Spirit is the principle of personal religious experience, of individual inspiration; as such, it is the never-exhausted discloser of "new truth."

3. THE FOURTH GOSPEL

As we move on from the first three Gospels and the Book of Acts to the Fourth Gospel, we discover ourselves in still another world. And in no respect more sharply and bafflingly

than in the place held by the Holy Spirit and the interpretation of it. As a matter of fact, John's interpretation is not
wholly consistent. There are two main strands here and these
cannot be readily reconciled.

In parts of the Gospel, the Spirit is a present Reality. It
illumines Jesus Himself: "God hath given him the Spirit
without measure" (3:34); here the thought is akin to that of
the biographical narratives of the Synoptic Gospels. Again,
Jesus is represented as summoning a chance acquaintance of
dubious morals to worship of that immediate Presence: "The
hour cometh, and now is, when the true worshippers shall
worship the Father in spirit and in truth. . . . God is a Spirit,
and they that worship him must worship him in spirit and in
truth" (4:23, 24)—a conception which might be held to stand
in the tradition of the 139th and 51st Psalms. Again, this
Spirit brings spiritual rebirth here and now to those to whom
it is given. (3:5; 6:63) It is like the wind which bloweth
where it listeth. (3:8) And Jesus declares that "The words
which I speak are Spirit and life." (6:63)

But Jesus' major and more characteristic teaching regarding the Spirit in the Fourth Gospel seems to be in direct contradiction. The Spirit is promised as the Counselor or
Comforter to be sent by the Father after Jesus is no longer
present—the Spirit of truth to testify of him and to reveal
all truth. (14:15-26; 15:26-27; 16:7-15)

Can these contrasted and seemingly conflicting strands of
tradition be brought into harmony? There would appear
to be only two possible alternative methods of reconciliation.

One accepts the view of some Johannine scholars that
the later chapters of this Gospel embody authentic reminis-
cences of Jesus' teaching during His last hours. If this view

be accepted, it implies that the Synoptic record faithfully sets forth Jesus' near-silence with respect to the Spirit during the greater part of His ministry and especially regarding the Spirit's relation to Himself and His vocation, but that as His end drew near, He was led to forecast the gift of the Spirit as Guide and Comforter for His disspirited followers in the glorious promises declared in the "Last Discourse" of John 14-16.

For the alternative explanation, the Synoptic record of Jesus' words, and it alone, truthfully reflects His own thought. The ascription of the pivotal events of His life to the Spirit, and the teaching regarding the Spirit attributed to Him in the Fourth Gospel, as well as, in all probability, most if not all the references to the Spirit in His mouth in the Synoptics, must be recognized as the interpretation of the Early Church, itself living within vivid experience of the Spirit, read back into earlier happenings including His teaching.

Certain corollaries follow, some of them with only indirect bearing upon our major concern but with challenging implications for the interpretation of Christian Faith in our time. I shall mention only two:

a. In our day, we stand in sharp reaction from an axiom of our immediate forebears which posited a distinction, unhappily phrased to be sure, between "the religion of Jesus" and "the religion about Jesus"; more accurately, between the faith of Jesus and the faith of the Early Church. The prevailing orthodoxy dismisses any such distinction as the construction of so-called Liberal Theology, to be banished with all its ideas as well as all its works. It is difficult to examine the New Testament dispassionately, especially what it says about the Holy Spirit, without recognizing that distinction, however we may phrase it. The personal faith of Jesus as revealed in His authentic words hardly acknowledges the Holy Spirit. The faith of the Early Church pivoted on the centrality of the Holy Spirit.

b. Another canon of contemporary interpretation delights to cast doubt on the reliability of the whole of the recorded teaching of Jesus. What our Gospels, even the Synoptics, present, we are informed, is not authentic recollections of Jesus' words but rather the sermonizing of the Early Church. Apart from all other evidence, it is hard to understand how such a thesis can stand in the face of one fact—the almost total absence of the Holy Spirit from the reported utterances of Jesus. In view of the pervasion of the thought of Early Christianity including its preaching by the conviction of the Holy Spirit, as testified by virtually every source, it surpasses credence that, if the words attributed to Jesus in the Synoptic Gospels were principally a reflection of Early Christian preaching, they likewise would not have been permeated by references to the Holy Spirit, as indeed are those parts of them which describe the events of Jesus' life rather than report His sayings. Conversely, it is amazing that these sayings have not been penetrated by such references, introduced inadvertently if not deliberately. Take Luke for illustration. The historian of the Primitive Church, whose account in Acts is dominated by the Spirit, in his companion volume of biography portrays the Spirit's work in furnishing the setting for Jesus' life but only thrice reports the Spirit on Jesus' lips, and two of these references are of doubtful accuracy. It would be difficult to imagine stronger and more objective evidence of the resolve of the Evangelists to render Jesus' actual words, and of their success.

The main conclusions, however, are two:

1. Jesus found no occasion for frequent reference to the Holy Spirit, certainly through the major part of his ministry. This is a startling conclusion, and its challenge must not be evaded. Perhaps He, like the Early Prophets, was repelled by crude conceptions of the Spirit in popular faith. Doubtless, Dr. Scott is right when he suggests:

> "We may well believe that it was not entirely congenial to his own mind. His sense of God was immediate and personal. He may have felt that an idea like that of the Spirit removed God to a distance, or put an abstract power in place of Him. . . . His silence on the Spirit would result unconsciously from the effort to think of God directly as the Father who was ever near to His children. . . .
> "His sense of fellowship with God was not an ecstasy to which he was subject at rare intervals, but his habitual mood. His insight into the will of God was calm and uninterrupted."[4]

2. In the faith of the Early Church, the Spirit was a central, perhaps *the* central reality. It was not primarily a conviction for thought, certainly not a matter of instructed dogma. It sprang directly from vivid, commanding, indubitable experience.

Conscientious Christian interpretation cannot evade that contrast. It lifts to primary importance the currently denied contrast between the faith of Jesus and the faith of Early Christianity.

[4] Scott, *op. cit.*, pp. 79, 80

4. PAUL

The experience of the Earliest Church furnished the atmosphere in which Paul came to Christian Faith. This was the setting for all his work. It is against the background of the conception of the Holy Spirit revealed in Acts rather than in the Gospels that Paul found himself led to wrestle with the nature and meaning of the Holy Spirit. It was in Paul's thought that the Christian understanding of the Holy Spirit was radically recast and came to its definitive fulfillment within the Bible; here is the true "telos," the authentic culmination of the pilgrimage which we have been tracing down the centuries.

As to the centrality of the Spirit for Paul, Sabatier does not exaggerate:

> "It is the soul of the doctrine, the binding principle which makes all its parts coherent ... a specific category of thought fixing the point of view from which the apostle carries on all his meditations and reasonings, coordinates and logically develops his entire conception of Christianity."[5]

And Wheeler Robinson voices a sound judgment when he declares:

> "The increasing recognition that the doctrine of the Holy Spirit is central in the Christian thought of the Apostle Paul (rather than the Rabbinical doctrine of

[5] August Sabatier, *The Religions of Authority and the Religion of the Spirit*, pp. 305 f.

'justification') marks a great advance in the interpretation of his Gospel."[6]

However, Paul's thought regarding the Spirit reveals marked development. Even within the brief time spanned by his letters, three periods stand forth sharply distinguished:—

1. In the earliest epistles, to the Thessalonians, "he scarcely exceeds the usual teaching of the first generation."[7] The Holy Spirit is the bestower of power, of joy, of moral purity, of religious consecration. (I, 1:5, 6; 4:8; II, 2:13) But also of extraordinary gifts of prophecy. (I, 5:19) The familiar outward marks of the Spirit's presence in ecstasy, etc., are recognized but not criticized.

2. In the great letters of the central period of Paul's ministry (Romans, Corinthians, Galatians), however, his understanding of the Holy Spirit appears to undergo a profound and far-reaching, indeed epoch-making, transformation. These alterations, as with almost any great creative mind, are doubtless due to two sets of pressures upon his thought, the one external, the other internal. On the one hand, deepening concern over the excesses attributed to the Spirit's influence among his fellow-Christians all about him troubled him increasingly. The writer of the Fourth Gospel must have felt the same disquiet, and sought to deal with it by linking the Spirit to Jesus' own teaching, placing in the Master's mouth specific descriptions of what the Spirit was to be and could be expected to do and say; his method and Paul's for curbing the same aberrations furnish an instructive study in similarity and in contrast. On the other hand, Paul's own experience appears to have enlarged and deepened steadily

[6] Robinson, *The Christian Experience of the Holy Spirit*, p. 14.
[7] H. B. Swete, *On the Early History of the Doctrine of the Holy Spirit*, p. 409.

and rapidly. The upshot was a profound revision of currently prevailing thought of the Spirit in three closely related respects.

a. Paul does not disavow spectacular manifestations of the Spirit's presence. On the contrary, he claims them in supreme degree for himself. But they are made secondary; more than that, they are brought under judgment of quite new and loftier norms. "Yet show I unto you a more excellent way. I may speak with the tongues of men and of angels, but if I have not love, I am a noisy gong or a clanging cymbal." (I Corinthians 12:30-13:1)

b. The tests of the authenticity of claimed-gifts of the Spirit are moral and ethical. More than that, the Holy Spirit, far from continuing as non-moral or sub-moral in its effects, becomes the very principle of the Christian's ethical life. For "the fruit of the Spirit is love, joy, peace, patience, kindness, goodness, faithfulness, gentleness, self-control." (Galatians 5:22-23) And, by its fruits shall it be known.

c. Finally and most important—the most original contribution of Paul to the Christian conception of the Holy Spirit if not to Christian Faith in its entirety, and the very center and fulcrum of Paul's own religion—the Holy Spirit is linked explicitly and indissolubly with Christ. For, "the Lord is that Spirit." And, "Where the Spirit of the Lord is, there is liberty." For, "we all, with unveiled face, beholding as in a mirror the glory of the Lord, are being changed into his likeness from one degree of glory to another; for this comes from the Lord who is the Spirit." (II Corinthians 3:17-18) Indeed, the Spirit is, above all, the agency of moral transformation ("sanctification"), and that transformation is into the likeness of Christ, because the Holy Spirit which is the Spirit of God *is* the Spirit of Christ. The radical and all-embracing character of this insight is revealed in the alternative use, as though interchangeable, of the variant terms "Spirit," "Spirit of God," "Spirit of Christ," "Holy Spirit"; so that, at the heart of that greatest of all the discourses of Paul which itself stands as the very pivot of all his thought, the eighth chapter of Romans, he declares confusingly but rightly, "Ye are not in the flesh, but in the Spirit, if so be that the Spirit of God dwell in you. Now if any man have not the Spirit of Christ, he is none of his." (Romans 8:9)[8] And then he adds the declaration which speaks as a succinct summary of the essence of both Old Testament and New Testament conviction with respect to the relation of the Spirit of God to spirit in man and of the latter to Christ: "The Spirit himself bears witness with our spirit that we are children of God, and if children, then heirs, heirs of God and fellow heirs (joint-heirs) with Christ." (Romans 8:16-17) Is anything more to be said of the very essence of Christian truth and faith?

This marks the loftiest summit of Paul's apprehension of the Holy Spirit. But if the later letters which have traditionally been attributed to Paul are really his, it is not his last word.

3. In the so-called "letters of his imprisonment" (Philippians, Ephesians, Colossians, the Pastorals), he adds to his earlier teaching a view of the relation of the Spirit to the Church for which, as we have seen, there was anticipation in Acts and in his own earlier epistles, although there it certainly had a subordinate importance. Now the Spirit is

---

[8] "Spirit," "Spirit of God," "Spirit of Christ" occur thirteen times in the first sixteen verses of this chapter.

set forth as the bond of Christian unity. Christians are to "endeavor to keep the unity of the Spirit in the bond of peace" because "there is one body and one Spirit." (Ephesians 4:3-4)

But this change of emphasis, like the claim that in Acts the Spirit is peculiarly the possession of the Church, can be and has been exaggerated. Setting aside the Pastorals as of doubtful Pauline authorship,[9] there is nothing in these last letters which is not wholly consonant with his greatest teaching; of course, there is only "one Spirit" and of course that Spirit must effect spiritual unity among those who are truly responsive to it.

Nevertheless, the major emphasis of the Letters of the Imprisonment as of their predecessors is not upon the role of the Spirit in the Church but of its action upon individuals. Take, for illustration, Ephesians, often held to be the Charter of Paul's doctrine of the Church. "We have access by one Spirit unto the Father." (2:18) Christians are to be "renewed in the spirit of their minds." (4:23) Part of their equipment for spiritual combat is to be "the sword of the Spirit which is the word of God." (6:17) This is the same Spirit as in the earlier letters to the Romans and Galatians. In the reading of Paul's climactic thought of the Spirit as wholly or principally a possession of the Church, it appears as though we again confront a familiar trick of interpretation—reading back into earlier teaching views which have become axiomatic for the later interpreters.

In this second transition, so far as it can be identified, Paul's thought is doubtless again under a double compulsion. On the one hand, positively, it reflects continuing growth in

---

[9] Many foremost New Testament scholars also question the Pauline authorship of Ephesians and certainly of Colossians.

his own apprehension. On the other hand, negatively, he is reacting to very concrete and troublous problems of his ministry—now, not primarily misbehavior of individual Christians, but rather strife and schism within the Christian fellowship. And, as with the aftermath in the Old Testament of the exalted vision of the great prophets, seers and psalmists, the question must be raised whether Paul's last word (if it really be his last word) represents culmination or anticlimax.

In any event, Paul's association of the Spirit with the Church well prepares us for the next stage in the Spirit's pilgrimage, in the hands of the Church theologians of the centuries. Henceforth, the key issue becomes: What is the relation of the Holy Spirit to the Church? How far is the Spirit confined in its operation to the Church? How far, and in what sense, does the Church possess the Spirit?

These questions will occupy us in the next chapter.

CHAPTER FOUR

THE CHURCH
THROUGH THE CENTURIES

A full account of the development of the doctrine of the
Holy Spirit in Christian Faith would involve us in a review
of the entire history of Christian thought; for this there is
neither time nor, fortunately, need. We must make choice
between such a comprehensive survey and a focusing of attention upon the major events of the chronicle. We gladly choose
the latter. For example, we may well pass over altogether
that protracted and involved dispute over "the procession of
the Holy Spirit"—whether the Holy Spirit is to be conceived
as deriving from both the Father and the Son or only from
the Father—which aligned theologians of East and West in
embattled phalanxes for centuries and proved the occasion,
though hardly the sole cause, of the first "great schism" in
Christendom. Doubtless there were values of moment at
stake in that controversy, as there almost always are in
theological conflict. But they were purely speculative in
nature, concerned with the inmost secrets of the Godhead.
They were certainly not of an import to justify a major and

lasting rift in the Body of Christ. In any event, they stand at far remove from our main concerns.

We may summarize the pilgrimage of the idea of the Holy Spirit through the Christian centuries in four episodes.

I. THE DEFINITION OF THE HOLY SPIRIT

The first period, running to about 400 A.D., culminated in the adoption of the official creedal interpretations of the Holy Spirit.

But the prior fact, to which we alluded in the first chapter, was the comparative absence of the Holy Spirit from theological attention from the close of the New Testament to the beginning of the Fourth Century. Of the fact itself, there can be no question. We quoted earlier the considered judgment of the foremost historian of thought concerning the Holy Spirit in the early centuries, Dr. H. B. Swete: "In the earliest age of the Church comparatively little attention was paid to the doctrine of the Holy Spirit."[1]

The major reason usually given for this inattention is that the mind of the Church was preoccupied with another more basic and important matter—the meaning of Christ and its interpretation. As the historian just quoted goes on to explain: "It [the doctrine of the Holy Spirit] was thrown into the background by the paramount importance of the doctrine of the Person of Christ."[2] This fact requires some qualification of the view that the Holy Spirit occupied the center of early Christian faith. If this was true of the Primitive Church portrayed in Acts, from Paul onward the faith of the Church

[1] H. B. Swete, *On the Early History of the Doctrine of the Holy Spirit*, p. 5.
[2] *Ibid.*

was indisputably Christo-centric. It was altogether appropriate, indeed inevitable, that Christian theology should have first given its attention to that fact, to christology.

However, Dr. Scott fastens upon the profounder explanation:

> "It is noteworthy that in the subsequent period, when the ecclesiastical idea had begun to overshadow all Christian thought, the belief in the Spirit tended to disappear, or to have a merely formal value. . . . The Spirit had meaning only so long as it acted directly on men as individuals, and when they could not receive it except through the church and its ordinances they lost the feeling of its reality."[3]

Nevertheless, even during this time of silence, two convictions concerning the Holy Spirit quietly and unobtrusively established themselves:

a. The kinship, indeed equality, of the Spirit with the Father and the Son. This resulted less from conscious reflection than from the well-nigh universal use of two Scriptural phrases at moments of peculiar sacredness in the worship of the Church. First, the "Great Commission" which concludes the Gospel of Matthew when the Risen Christ enjoins His followers to go into all the world and make disciples of all nations, "baptizing them in the name of the Father and of the Son and of the Holy Spirit" (28:19); this provided the Church with the formula repeated at the admission of new members through baptism. Second, the "Great Benediction" with which Paul had concluded his Second Letter to the Corinthians; this early established the pre-eminence it has

[3] E. F. Scott, *The Spirit in the New Testament*, pp. 125, 126.

enjoyed ever since as the favorite blessing at the close of Christian worship: "The grace of the Lord Jesus Christ, and the love of God, and the communion of the Holy Spirit, be with you all." (13:14) These devotional uses found creedal embodiment in the Old Roman Symbol, which also early became the most authoritative summary of the Faith as the "Apostles' Creed"; and so Christians affirmed their belief, not only in "God the Father Almighty, Maker of heaven and earth," and in "Jesus Christ, his only Son, our Lord," but also in "the Holy Spirit," though they added nothing to indicate who or what the Holy Spirit was understood to be and do.

b. The second conviction followed from the first. As the Christian mind battled its way through the whirlpools and rapids of sharp controversy to its definite affirmation at the Council of Nicaea in 325 that Christ must be regarded as fully divine, "of the same substance with the Father," the deity of the Holy Spirit was assumed and accepted by implication, without dispute and almost without consideration.

In these first three centuries, at only one point was there speculation concerning the Holy Spirit which might have had decisive effect on all subsequent thought. As the Church fastened upon the term "Logos," universally prevalent throughout that Graeco-Roman world, and sought to incorporate it within Christian vocabularies, there were those who proposed that the Logos should be recognized by Christian Faith as the philosophic term for the Holy Spirit. We have already noted this possibility in the period between the Old and New Testaments, and have suggested its logical persuasion and its great promise of enrichment for Christian Faith.[4]

As a matter of fact, this was a widely prevalent, perhaps

[4] See above, Chapter 2, p. 49.

the predominant, assumption among the earliest theologians, known in Church History as "The Apostolic Fathers." Dr. Swete summarizes their usage: "It is common to find the titles of the Holy Ghost assigned to the Logos."[5] Ignatius of Antioch, Aristides, the First Epistle of Clement, the Epistle of Barnabas, the Second Epistle of Clement, the Shepherd of Hermas—all, either in explicit statements or by implication, appear to have identified the preexistent Christ with the Holy Spirit. For example, the Shepherd of Hermas declares that "that Spirit is the Son of God."[6] This whole complex matter, sometimes obscure and not always wholly consistent, has been given exhaustive and authoritative reinvestigation in a recent volume by Professor Harry A. Wolfson of Harvard who comes to this conclusion:

> "By the end of the period of the Apostolic Fathers, there was no belief in a preexistent Trinity. The Trinity of God, Christ, and the Holy Spirit began to them, with the birth of Jesus and continued after his resurrection and ascension. Before his birth there were only two preexistent beings, God and the Holy Spirit, the latter identified with the preexistent Christ, and, if the term Logos is used, it is identified with the Holy Spirit."[7]

Dr. Wolfson continues:

> "Beginning with the Apologists, however, a distinction is made between the preexistent Logos and the preexistent Holy Spirit, the former alone being identified with the preexistent Christ. The Holy Spirit becomes a

[5] H. B. Swete, *op. cit.,* p. 15.
[6] *Hermas,* Sim. V, 6, 5.
[7] Harry A. Wolfson, *The Philosophy of the Church Fathers,* Cambridge: Harvard University Press, Chapter XI, p. 191.

third preexistent incorporeal being, with the result that the Trinity, now a Trinity of God, the Logos and the Holy Spirit, no longer begins with the birth of Jesus; it has an existence prior to his birth and even prior to the creation of the world."[8]

The reasons for this change in conception of the relation of the Holy Spirit to the Logos and to the preexistent Christ were several. Many of them rooted back in the thought of Philo. Already in pre-Christian speculation, the Logos had become linked in men's minds with the Hebraic category of Wisdom or Word rather than with that of Spirit. This marriage persisted. Quite probably, the ill-repute of the strongest advocate of the identification of Logos with Spirit, Paul of Samosata, that brilliant mind branded heretic, cast such a suggestion into disfavor. And the Fourth Gospel seemed to support the alternative linkage of Logos and Christ and to recognize no connection between the Logos of its Prologue and the Spirit who is mentioned in the two seemingly inconsistent senses which we noted above.[9] Even more influential, doubtless, was the devotional use of the Baptismal formula and the Great Benediction.

But consider how different would have been the outcome if the Prologue to the Fourth Gospel had been read: "In the beginning was the Spirit, and the Spirit was with God, and the Spirit was God. . . . All things were made by him. . . . In him was life and the life was the light of men. . . . And the Spirit became flesh and dwelt among us, full of grace and truth." Such a rendering might have claimed far closer fidelity both to the generally prevailing meaning of Logos

[8] Wolfson, op. cit., p. 191.
[9] See above, Chapter 3, pp. 60 f.

in the thought of the time and to the historic connotation of the Spirit throughout Scripture, notably the account of creation in Genesis 1, but also Paul's glorious portrayal of the Spirit in Romans, 8.[10] But this was not to be.

The Church, having categorically established the full deity of Christ at Nicaea in 325 though still merely declaring its belief in the Holy Spirit without elucidation, as in the Apostles' Creed, finally "got around" to consider what it understood by the Holy Spirit. Sometime between the early draft of the Nicene Creed of 325 and its final formulation authorized by the second "ecumenical" Council of Constantinople in 381, fifty-six years later, there were added these descriptive phrases: "The Holy Spirit, the Lord, the life-giver, which proceedeth from the Father, which with the Father and the Son is worshipped and glorified, which spake through the prophets." The additions were strictly scriptural. Paul in II Corinthians 3:17 had declared, "The Lord is that Spirit." The Fourth Evangelist had proclaimed, "It is the Spirit that gives life," (6:63) and later had added, "The Comforter will come, whom I will send you from the Father." (15:26) In the perspective of Church History, these phrases have a special interest because one of them, "which proceedeth from the Father," furnished the battle-ground for theological disputation which eventuated nearly seven centuries later in the separation of Eastern from Western Christendom. But from the point of view of the development of doctrine, their importance lies in the fact that they determined for all time the official Christian definition of the Holy Spirit.

---

[10] Cp. Wheeler Robinson's similar suggestion in a casual footnote: "It is interesting to speculate on the consequences for Christian theology if the Logos idea had been linked to the Spirit instead of the Son." *The Christian Experience of the Holy Spirit*, p. 21n.

There they stand, authoritative to this day: "The Holy Spirit is the Lord, the life-giver, which proceedeth from the Father (*or* the Father and the Son; so Augustine and Western Christendom), which with the Father and the Son is to be worshipped and glorified, which spake through the prophets"![11]

2. THE HOLY SPIRIT AND THE CHURCH

At about 400, we pass to the second main period which continues to the Protestant Reformation.

The Niceno-Constantinopolitan Creed, as so often is the consequence of precise theological formulation, precipitated almost more problems than it settled. But, sharp and divisive as they proved to be, they were occupied almost wholly with purely speculative assertions regarding the relations of the Spirit to the Father and the Son; that is, they were attempts to penetrate the inmost being of the Godhead. We may properly defer attention to them until we return to these ultimate and most difficult questions in our last chapter.

For our interest, the central theme of the second period is on a much more accessible level. It is concerned with the relations of the Holy Spirit, not to other realities within the Godhead, but to the very mundane reality of the Christian Church.

The complex of causes which led, in the centuries following the New Testament, to the emergence and crystallization of three correlative instruments of church discipline—scrip-

---

[11] Severe strictures upon the adequacy of this creedal description of the Holy Spirit have recently been levelled by Prof. Hendry because of its failure to link the Holy Spirit with Christ (*The Holy Spirit in Christian Theology*, p. 9). Cp. the contrary appraisal of Swete, *op. cit.*, pp. 90 ff.

ture-canon, creed, and episcopacy—are well known. Some were external, such as defense against misrepresentation and persecution. Some were internal, mainly the felt-need for exclusion of heresy and repression of disorder. One of the most troublesome factors on both scores, discrediting Christianity in the eyes of outsiders and disturbing the "good order" of the Church's life, was unquestionably the beliefs and behaviors attributed to the direction of the Holy Spirit.

We have already had occasion to note the almost unfailing aftermath of any vibrant and dynamic outpouring of the Holy Spirit. Two independent factors conspire to the same end: on the one hand, slackening of vitality in the experience of the Spirit's presence; on the other hand, alarm over the more extreme effects of the Spirit's activity. Moreover, it must be recognized that, as dynamic power slackens, excesses of both interpretation and expression tend to aggravate.

The first of these sequels—loss of a vital awareness of the Spirit—followed upon the highest ascents of realization of the Spirit in the Old Testament, to issue in the spiritual low-lands of the pre-New Testament period. It occurred again in the post-New Testament epoch. We have already quoted Dr. Scott's explanation of the earlier illustration: "Belief in the Spirit has its ground in certain experiences, and in the religion of the later age these had become unusual, and to a great extent unreal";[12] and of the later instance: "In the subsequent period, when the ecclesiastical idea had begun to overshadow all Christian thought, the belief in the Spirit tended to disappear, or to have a merely formal value."[13]

We have also observed how the second of these mutually

[12] Scott, *op. cit.*, p. 47.
[13] *Ibid.*, p. 125.

supporting factors—alarm over the extreme manifestations of the Spirit—dissuaded the early prophets altogether from associating themselves with claims to the Spirit's inspiration; and, again, how both the Fourth Evangelist and the Apostle Paul strove to curb license in the Spirit's name. The instrument on which they relied was purification and elevation of men's thoughts about the Spirit by linking the Holy Spirit to Christ. But their efforts were by no means wholly successful; aberrations, claimed to be the work of the Holy Spirit, continued to disrupt the Church's peace, stain its purity and embarrass its leaders. Moreover, professional ecclesiasts constitutionally distrust the novel, the unconventional and, even more, the reproachful and the challenging. The corrective of internal purification seems to them too precarious and too gentle; they incline toward the sterner surety of external control. They may seek to discredit and disown what they distrust, as did Amos and Micah; or they may accomplish the same end by taking the troublesome disturber under their patronage and emasculating it through redefinition and regulation.

It was, therefore, inevitable that the leaders of the Catholic Church, rapidly developing its structure, its order, its discipline and its respectability, should find themselves under the necessity of dealing with the operations of the Holy Spirit. The problem occupied them, off and on, for some fifteen centuries. Moreover, the outcome of that dealing was likewise so inevitable that a sage observer of human institutions, especially those making claim to divine authority, might have forecast it from the outset.

First, Scripture was recognized as the official repository of the Holy Spirit's utterances; thereby, the written record was invested with divine authority, and the divine inspiration was confined within records from the past.

But who could rightly understand and interpret Scripture and draw authoritative corollaries? Gregory the Great maintained that general Councils of the Church were especially inspired by the Holy Spirit. The weighty Council of Trent (1545-1563), confronted by the Protestant rebellion, decreed that "unwritten traditions of the Church were of equal authority with written Scriptures, since they had come down in unbroken succession from the apostles, who had received them from the mouth of Christ himself or from the Holy Spirit's dictation." The logical *finis*, or, as Protestants would hold, the *reductio ad absurdum,* was delayed until the Vatican Council of 1870 which pronounced it as "a divinely revealed dogma" that "when the Roman pontiff speaks *ex cathedra* . . . by the Divine assistance promised him in the blessed Peter, he possesses that power of infallibility with which the Divine Redeemer willed that His Church should be furnished in defining doctrine on faith or morals." At long last the Holy Spirit has become in truth the bondsman of the Church which claims its origin in the Spirit's creative action.

3. CLASSIC PROTESTANTISM

It might have been expected that the Protestant revolt of Luther and Calvin, dedicated to the recovery of the true faith including the freedom of the Christian man, would have reclaimed authentic freedom for the Holy Spirit. But it is becoming increasingly recognized, at long last, that classic Protestantism was far from the thorough-going revolution which tradition has pictured, and that its reclamation of original Christianity was far from radical and complete. To be sure, both Luther and Calvin laid hold of the principle of the Spirit's inward operation upon the souls of believers.

> "I believe that it is not of my own reason or by my own strength that I believe in Jesus Christ my Lord: it is the Holy Ghost that by the Gospel has called me, with His gifts has enlightened me, through genuine faith has sanctified and sustained me, just as He calls, gathers together, enlightens, sanctifies, and sustains by Jesus Christ, in true faith, all Christendom."[14]

> "The Holy Spirit is the bond by which Christ efficaciously binds us to himself," creating faith "by which the believer receives Christ; where the Spirit illumines to faith, Christ inserts us within His Body and we become partakers of all goods."[15]

But, both Luther and Calvin were essentially cautious and, after the manner of most great reformers, increasingly conservative with advancing years and experience. For Luther, that which, in his lovely phase, "the Holy Ghost writes inwardly in the heart" came to be confined to the teaching of Scripture which Luther held to be "the book, writing and word of the Holy Spirit." And Calvin's no less lofty and moving *testimonium spiritus sancti internum,* the inward testimony of the Holy Spirit, was likewise held to confine its persuasion to the truth of Scripture. Thus, the way was prepared for later Protestant legalism and scholasticism, based upon the inerrancy of the texts of the Old and New Testaments.

[14] Martin Luther, *Cat. Min.,* art. iii.
[15] John Calvin, *Institutes,* Book III, Ch. i, #1,4; Ch. ii, #35.

4. RADICAL PROTESTANTISM

Nevertheless, the great spiritual revolution of the Sixteenth Century was not without recovery of the Scripture's own teaching regarding the Holy Spirit and its operation.

It was left to the despised Anabaptists to claim that the inward voice of the Holy Spirit takes precedence over the external word of Scripture, or the dicta of prelate. As in earlier periods, the claim was employed to justify all manner of ideas and behavior which outraged the theologians and scandalized the ecclesiasts. But also, once again, the Holy Spirit was emancipated from the leading-strings of dogma and the dead-hand of tradition to resume its guidance of the minds and hearts of the devout into new truth.

And, in later, more sophisticated and more responsible interpretation at the hands of Friends, Congregationalists, Moravians and Methodists, the Holy Spirit came afresh upon Christians to revive, to re-empower, and to thrust them forth across the face of the earth to carry the Good News of the transforming present power of the Spirit of Christ which is the Spirit of God which is the Holy Spirit to every continent and race and nation, almost to every creature, for the fulfillment of their Lord's final command "to teach all nations." It is still too little recognized how largely the epoch-making renewals of the Eighteenth and Nineteenth Centuries were direct fruitage of the recovery of a true understanding of the Holy Spirit. Jonathan Edwards' biographer reminds us that: "The impulse of the Great Awakening was a theological conviction which took shape in Edwards' mind, a belief in the immediate action of the Divine Spirit upon the human soul."[16]

There is no more convincing evidence of the ultimate fruitage of Radical Protestantism's recovery of the Holy Spirit than this simple fact: Of the missionary outreach of the past century and a half—by general acknowledgment, the most mighty achievement of the Church in behalf of its Lord in the whole nineteen centuries—over half was the work of Christian groups born, directly or indirectly, of Radical Protestantism. There is even more striking evidence in the fact that, of the total allegiance to Christ represented today in the World Council of Churches, almost half belong to the so-called "Free Churches"—Baptists, Methodists, Congregationalists, Disciples and lesser children of the "radical" wing of the Reformation.

5. IN SUMMARY

Now, from this long, and at some points unavoidably complicated, biography, can we distill any general conclusions?

1. The first is the well-nigh universal recognition of the reality of the Holy Spirit—a finding already established in our wider survey of the religious life of mankind, underscored from Jewish-Christian history. Time and again—in pre-Christian Hebraism, in the first Christian centuries, and all through the pilgrimage of the Church—the Holy Spirit has been both distrusted and neglected. Always, it has reappeared and reasserted its role as the Living and Potent Agent of God for the purification and empowerment of His children—*God-near* and *God-at-work*.

[16] A. V. G. Allen, *Jonathan Edwards*, p. 134.

2. When awareness of the Spirit has grown dim, men have either relegated its activity to times past *or* to an Age of the Spirit yet to come.

3. Each fresh outpouring of the Spirit has been fraught with perils and has bequeathed problems. Always, it appears to lay such mighty hold upon men's imaginations, to stir so profoundly their emotions and their wills, that they are tempted to excesses and aberrations; and they yield to these temptations. Always, it requires curbing and demands discipline.

4. The perplexities and problems thus created for the guardians of tradition and good order have led them to two alternative expedients in dealing with their troublesome disturber. Some of the noblest have ignored the Spirit altogether. But the more usual method of handling this innovator and upsetter of the status quo has been to bring it under their own direction and control—either by making its Voice subservient to ecclesiastical interpretation *or* by limiting its authentic speech to the recorded writings of the past. Thus, we see: the Holy Spirit is not only the point of contact between Christianity and other faiths. Within Christianity, it is the heart of the issues between Catholicism and Protestantism, and between both Classical Catholicism and Classical Protestantism on the one hand and Radical Protestantism on the other hand. That is to say, a correct understanding of the Holy Spirit is the crucial issue in the Doctrine of the Church. And it is a commonplace among students of the divisions of Christendom that the differences which divide Christians into separated Churches all center in their divergent Doctrines of the Church.[17]

[17] Cf. Henry P. Van Dusen, *World Christianity: Yesterday, Today and Tomorrow*, Chapter 8.

5. The right and true solution of the "problem of the Spirit" lies in none of these directions. It lies in bringing men's claims of inspiration or possession of the Holy Spirit into subjection to Christ. It lies in taking with utmost seriousness and fullest acceptance the noblest insight of the greatest interpreter of this as of so many other truths of Christian Faith—the Apostle Paul—that "the Lord is that Spirit," for the Spirit which is the Holy Spirit which is the Spirit of God is—THE SPIRIT OF CHRIST.

PART THREE

SPIRIT,
SON
AND
FATHER

From even so summary a review of the Holy Spirit in the religious consciousness of mankind, and, more particularly, within the Hebraic-Christian tradition, certain conclusions stand forth:

1. The concept of Divine Spirit is not an exclusively or even distinctively Christain conviction. In some form, not without at least superficial similarity to Christian thought, it appears in many religions, both of the ancient and of the modern worlds. The common elements in the idea within the several religions are: the Divine Spirit is an influence or emanation given forth or proceeding from the Ultimate Divine Being, usually marked by the bestowal of exceptional powers, and closely related to the life of man. It denotes—God Present and God Active.

2. In Hebraic faith, Spirit holds a large place. "Spirit" is the principle of life in both Nature and man. Two features characterize almost all references to the Divine Spirit—intimacy and potency. The Spirit of God is—God-near and God-at-work.

3. In the New Testament, the Holy Spirit (in the Old Testament so designated only twice, but in climactic passages) is virtually absent from the indubitably authentic words of Jesus, but is closely associated with most of the crucial events in the life of Jesus. It is given definite meaning by the Apostle Paul, primarily through linkage of the Holy Spirit with Christ; Spirit which is the Holy Spirit which is the Spirit of God is the Spirit of Christ. Thereby, thought of the Spirit is ethicized; its unfailing fruits are love, joy, peace, patience, kindness, goodness, faithfulness, gentleness, self-control; the greatest of these is love; and by its fruits is it to be known. Likewise, the Holy Spirit is the indwelling reality of the Christian's life; to dwell in Christ is to have Christ dwell in the heart by faith; and to be in Christ is to be in the Spirit and to have the Spirit dwell within one, sanctifying the whole of life and guiding it into all truth.

4. In the history of Christian thought, the Holy Spirit becomes peculiarly associated with, first, Scripture, and then the Church; thus it furnishes the crux of the debate between Catholicism and Protestantism. But the Radical Reformation challenged the contention that the Holy Spirit confines its operation wholly or principally to Scripture or Church or both, and maintained that it is primarily the agency of God's self-disclosure to the individual Christian in his inmost soul; thus the Holy Spirit becomes the key point of differentiation between Catholicism and Classic Protestantism on the one hand and free or radical or sectarian Protestantism on the other hand. In summary, the Holy Spirit is the principle of authority in Christian Faith; and the central issue is whether authority resides, solely or ultimately or mainly, in a) Scripture, or b) Church, or c) conscience.

From these conclusions, arise certain basic questions:

1. What is the relation of the Holy Spirit to the Divine influence in Nature and in natural man? This, I would suggest, is the soundest and most significant perspective for an examination of God's relation to Nature, i.e., of natural religion and natural theology.

2. What is the relation of the Holy Spirit in Hebraic-Christian faith to the Divine Spirit in other religions? Is the relation primarily one of kinship or of contrast, of continuity or of radical discontinuity? This, I would urge, is both the most suggestive and most fruitful context for a consideration of the right relationship of Christianity and other religions.

3. What is the relation of the Holy Spirit in authentic and consummatory Christian Faith to earlier apprehensions of the Holy Spirit within Judaism and within primitive Christianity? This, I would propose, is perhaps the most promising setting for a study both of the much-debated subject of revelation, and of the development of Christian thought.

4. What is the relation of the Holy Spirit to the two other "Persons" of the Christian Trinity, to God the Father and to Jesus Christ? Since this is the issue upon which the first great schism in Christendom was precipitated—the separation of East and West—it is the necessary focus for consideration of the contrast between Eastern Orthodoxy and Western Christianity, whether Catholic or Protestant.

5. What is the relation of the Holy Spirit to a) Scripture, b) Church, and c) individual experience? As we have just observed, here is the heart of the divergence of Classic Protestantism from Catholicism, and of Radical Protestantism from both; and, therefore, the proper axis for discussions of the relative authenticity and authority of the principal alternative Western Christian traditions.

6. Lastly, what is the relation of the Holy Spirit to the other major elements within Christian belief? Here we are not in the first instance reposing the speculative questions which have so largely occupied the classic theologians—the relation of the Holy Spirit to the Father and the Son within the Godhead. Rather, we are raising the very practical and vital query: What, if any, is the bearing of Christian thought of the Holy Spirit upon the Christian understanding of man, of Christ, of God, of the Church?

Thus, we see what Christians believe about the Holy Spirit is involved in virtually every major problem of Christian faith. To be sure, as we suggested at the outset, such a discovery is implicit in the basic premise of a true Christian interpretation, namely, the recognition that all the elements in Christian belief are so intimately connected with each other that to examine any one of them thoroughly and adequately is to discover oneself compelled to consider all the others. This is a truism for a proper "systematic" or better "organic" theology. But the central contention of this book is far bolder and less conventional than that. It is: that the Holy Spirit is the fulcrum of all aspects of religious faith, and, therefore, the one best ground for consideration of the vast complex of issues just listed—natural religion, revelation, the relations of Christianity to other religions, and of the various divergent and sometimes contradictory understandings of Christian Faith to one another. And that this is so because the Holy Spirit concerns, above all, man's experience of the Divine, or conversely, the Divine's impact upon the souls of men; it is God-near and God-at-work; it is the meeting-place of the Divine and the human.

Obviously, space forbids exploration of all these many and

diverse themes, though we shall continue to hold them in mind and shall try to say something upon most of them. But we shall center attention upon the last question raised: the relation of the Holy Spirit to the other major elements within Christian belief. More specifically, we shall make bold to pose the query: what, if any, light is cast by Christian thought of the Holy Spirit upon the Christian understanding of man, of Christ, of God, and of the Church?

CHAPTER FIVE

THE HOLY SPIRIT
AND MAN

What illumination, if any, does the Holy Spirit bring to the Christian understanding of man?

The Holy Spirit casts helpful light upon our understanding of man at two places; so to say, at opposite poles of the Christian interpretation of man—its starting-point and its conclusion; our conception of man's beginning—his given nature, and our vision of man's destiny—his ideal end.

I.

In the biographical sketch of the pilgrimage of the idea of Spirit through the Hebraic-Christian tradition, we noted that, in its first beginnings far back on the dim border-land of pre-history, Spirit was thought of not as the principle of spiritual life, that which distinguishes man from the rest of animate nature, or even as the source of life itself, that which distinguishes man-as-animal from inanimate nature, but as energy at work throughout all Nature. Only later, though

still very early within our records, was Spirit in all its manifestations attributed to Divine Activity; Spirit is now the
Spirit of God. And, as the evidences of Spirit throughout
Nature were traced to the Divine Spirit as their source, so
that same Divine Spirit was recognized as the bestower of
spirit upon man. Perhaps our most trustworthy authority
upon early Hebraic anthropology, Dr. Wheeler Robinson,
declares: "The careful study of the Old Testament in its true
chronological order will reveal that as 'wind' became 'Spirit'
in relation to God, so 'Spirit' (i.e. Divine Spirit) became
'spirit' in man."[1]

It is well that we should accept and not disavow this primitive Hebraic insight, for it affirms what is as necessary for
true thought about man as it is valuable in inducing true
humility in man—that we are rooted in Nature, bone of inanimate nature's bone, but also flesh of animate nature's flesh.
Our passions have their sources in those of the beasts, from
whom we are sprung, and they never permit us to forget or
deny that lowly origin. So, also, our affections and our fidelities—even the loftiest of them such as parental concern or
group loyalty or readiness for self-sacrifice—have their anticipations in the highest levels of animal life. He who created
us created all; and He who breathed the breath of life into
man to constitute him a living soul did not withhold His life-
bestowing Spirit from any part of His creation. This is the
fountain-source of Natural Theology; and it is of the essence
of our Faith.

The Christian view of man begins—though it certainly
does not end—with the story of man's creation as man. The
more primitive account of creation in the second chapter of

[1] Robinson, *The Christian Experience of the Holy Spirit*, p. 13.

Genesis stands, in some respects, on a far lower plane than
the much later account which precedes it in our Bibles, in
the first chapter of Genesis. But it focusses on one declaration:
"The Lord God breathed the breath of life [His own Divine
Breath] into man's inanimate body, and man became a
living soul." (Genesis 2:7) That is to say, the Divine Breath
or Spirit (ruäḥ) is the very principle, the cause and secret,
of man's spiritual being or soul. This is the earlier creation
story's version of the later and loftier account's interpretation
of the origin of man: "And God said, Let us make man in
our image, after our likeness. . . . So God created man
in his own image, in the image of God created he him."
(Genesis 1:26-27)

Few topics have more divided theologians, and never more
than in our own day, than the *imago dei*. What is it? How is
it to be identified? And how defined?

There have been those who have sought to locate the
"image of God" in *man's rational faculties*—the powers of
memory, of anticipation, and of reason which seem most
sharply to mark him off from the rest of animate creation.
But, happily for man's humility, vast as is the difference in
degree between man and the highest animals in these respects, it does not appear possible to establish a sharp dividing-
line; for certain of the higher apes display quite extraordinary
powers of reasoning, while we marvel at the phenomenal
gifts of memory in birds, for example their always inexplicable and well-nigh unbelievable "homing instinct," and
of anticipation in most animals' shrewd provisions against
future needs. And the fact that these traits are apparently
rooted within the instincts, at a level far sub-human, does not
alter their character or diminish their marvel. All this is
strong confirmation from Nature for a true Christian view's

firm refusal to find the secret of man in his rational faculties, since it is the pure in heart not the clever of intellect who know God, and it is given to the child-like to comprehend what is hidden from the wise.

Others have discovered the "image of God" in the noblest in *man's emotional life*—his affections and fidelities and capacity for self-abnegation. But this identification is likewise denied by the presence of these same traits in almost the whole range of animal creation—however elemental their expression and even instinctive their dynamic.

Still another view finds the "image of God" in the *moral consciousness,* the categorical imperative to duty, which Immanuel Kant made the pivot of his philosophy and one pillar of his belief in God. Here we are on higher ground and closer to a tradition whose earliest law spoke in a series of commands, "thou shalt and thou shalt not," and whose final obedience is "to do the Will of God." But, here, likewise, there are sub-human anticipations. Even those fish which, in response to a categorical imperative lodged in their instincts, sacrifice their lives that another generation may have life are obeying a law of Nature which imposes upon them an irresistible command. And the St. Bernard dogs who hazard death for man's succour are not without some dim sense of duty. In training animals to abstain from brutality to their kind, as in training children to restrain *their* sadistic impulses, we are seeking to inculcate habits which advance beyond blind obedience to external authority to "reverence for life."

We are led closer to the truth by the interpretation, most fully and persuasively urged in our day by Dr. Emil Brunner,[2]

[2] See his essay in the Oxford Conference volume on *The Christian Understanding of Man,* and his fuller exposition in *Man in Revolt.*

that the *imago dei* is, specifically, *man's awareness of God* as One demanding the complete surrender of his life. For there appears to be no evidence whatever that even the most developed animals recognize a higher Power beyond Nature and man; though of course there is also no evidence, and probably never can be final proof, that such an awareness is nowhere present except in man.

But, the fontal account of the "image of God" in Genesis 1 and 2, upon which all subsequent speculation as to the *imago dei* in Christian theology is grounded, assumes a far more intimate lodgment of the Divine within man than is implied in the capacity to recognize and respond to God, priceless in its significance as that is. Dr. Brunner states:

> "The Bible expresses the distinctive quality of man by saying that he stands in a special relation to God, that the relation between God and man is that of "over-againstness"; that it consists in being face to face with each other.…
>
> "It is his relation to God which makes man man. This is the content of the Biblical doctrine of the *imago dei*."[3]

Dr. Brunner is surely right in saying that the Bible affirms "that man stands in a special relation to God" and that "it is his relation to God which makes man man." He is surely mistaken in adding that "the relation is that of 'over-againstness.'" On the contrary, the earlier account of the origin of man in Genesis declares that God breathed His own breath into man. Dr. Brunner's ingrained distrust of mysticism prevents him from taking this Biblical account at its face and true value. Authentic Christian thought recognizes that God

[3] Emil Brunner, in *The Christian Understanding of Man*, pp. 158, 159.

has lodged within man something of His own Being, His Spirit, so that the basic relation of God and man is not "over-againstness" but rather kinship of essential nature. This recognition has profound implications for all the rest of our thought of man, especially his salvation.

In summary, the "image of God" in man is that bestowal of Divine Spirit which, because it is God's gift of His own Spirit, has the capacity to recognize Him Who has made him and Whose he is. But sound reflection confirms our spiritual forbears' intuition that it is that same Divine Spirit which "moved upon the face of the deep" to bring the cosmos into being and which sustains all that it has made. Moreover, the works of that Spirit, as well as the Spirit itself in direct contact, may touch and stir its own "reflection" (i.e., "image") lodged within man's nature to recognize and respond ("through Nature to Nature's God"); just as a creative artist's writing or painting may stir response which should lead thought and recognition and gratitude through the author's or painter's handiwork to their creator, although this is always less satisfactory and less authoritative than direct personal intercourse when "spirit with spirit can meet."

Such "lodgment" of Divine Spirit within man is, as both tales of creation in Genesis imply, common to all men everywhere. And of that truth, the well-nigh universal "sense of the Divine" is empirical verification.[4] Here, then, is the elemental meeting-point of all religion and the proper starting-point for a comparative study of the faiths of mankind.

---

[4] An able and stimulating discussion of the relation of the Holy Spirit to the "image of God" in man is to be found in Dr. George S. Hendry's *The Holy Spirit in Christian Theology*, Chapter V: "The Holy Spirit and the Human Spirit." Dr. Hendry likewise finds the secret of the *imago dei* in the bestowal of God's Spirit, though he doubtless would not be prepared to draw all of the same conclusions from that premise. See especially pp. 106-107.

However, that initial gift of Spirit in man's creation does not represent the last initiative of God with respect to man's soul but only the first. Sound logic, no less than the testimony of the saints, declares that that living Spirit, which has created and even now pervades and sustains all, must be ceaselessly active seeking to draw those in whom He has been pleased to place His Spirit into ever fuller communion of spirit with Himself. And so, the proper destiny of man, dictated by his given nature in creation, is—unity of spirit, human spirit with Divine Spirit. Given kinship furnishes the ground for, and finds fulfillment in, communion. Thus we are carried directly to the far pole of the Christian interpretation of man—*man's ideal end*.

2.

Here, again, we confront variant interpretations. One, in particular, deserves our special attention. Starting, in true fidelity to the highest Hebrew conception, with God as Righteous Sovereign Whose Law demands man's unconditional obedience, Whose Purposes require for their fulfillment man's dedicated co-operation, and in Whose Will is to be discovered man's peace, this interpretation posits the highest relationship of God and man in terms of *will*, the surrender of man's will to the Divine Will, made possible by the gift of grace and issuing in full alignment of human purpose with Divine Design. This is a reading of human destiny so lofty that it seems impossible to go beyond it, as it is so right and necessary that nothing should be said which threatens to qualify it or relax its categorical obligation. Yet, it has been a sound instinct to which the mystics have been especially sensitive which has discerned that this interpretation envisions the ideal Divine-human relation in terms too external, as it tends to think of God in ideas too exclusively and narrowly anthropomorphic. It requires not to be displaced but to be supplemented by ways of thinking which, without imperiling either the transcendent holiness of God or the fully personal (better, supra-personal) character of His Being or the ethical stringency of His commands, introduces into our thought of his Intention for man's destiny that same quality of intimacy and immediacy which we have noted as an unfailing characteristic of the Divine Spirit's influence in man's creation. That is to say: It needs to be permeated by recognition of God's Holy Spirit.

This necessity comes home upon us when we examine more closely man's own nature. Speaking of the "essential difference between moral freedom and the freedom of the spirit," Professor George Thomas has written:

> "The moral will is the self moving towards a good that is not yet attained but is capable of being realized by action. Its freedom is an effortful freedom. Will is the initiative of the self, burdened by the limitations of the self. But *the spirit* is the self opening itself to universal truth and loving universal good. The spirit's activity is not initiated with painful effort but lured by the appeal of a higher life. . . . It is self forgetting and rising above self. It is not so much self striving for the universal as self laid hold of by the universal. Thus spiritual freedom is that which is achieved through devotion to universal truth and good."[5]

[5] George F. Thomas, *Spirit and Its Freedom*, pp. 110, 111.

For the abstract terms "universal truth" and "universal good," substitute the personal terms of Christian Faith and we have a good account of "Christian freedom": "The spirit is the self opening itself to the Divine Spirit . . . It is not so much self striving for God as self laid hold of by God's Holy Spirit. Thus spiritual freedom is that which is achieved through devotion to [better, possession by] the Holy Spirit." This is His service which is "perfect freedom."

Inevitably, our minds are drawn back to Paul's mighty *confessio fidei* in the seventh and eighth chapters of Romans:

> "The good that I would, I do not: but the evil that I would not, that I do. . . . Who shall deliver me from the body of this death? Thanks be to God through Jesus Christ our Lord! . . . For the law of the Spirit of life in Christ Jesus has set me free. . . . To set the mind on the Spirit is life and peace. . . . You are in the Spirit if the Spirit of God really dwells in you. If Christ is in you, your spirits are alive. . . . If the Spirit of Him who raised Jesus from the dead dwells in you, He who raised Christ Jesus from the dead will give life to your mortal bodies also through His Spirit which dwells in you. . . . For all who are led by the Spirit of God are sons of God. . . . The Spirit Himself bears witness with our spirit that we are children of God." (Romans 7:15-8:16)

All this is so because the Spirit is the Holy Spirit, that is the Spirit of God, which is the Spirit of Christ.

This modification or supplementation of "will" by "spirit" thus greatly enriches and empowers our thought of the Christian life. It has even more profound consequences for the interpretation of Christ, to which we shall shortly return.

3.

Paul's great exposition in Romans 8 is, of course, set against the background of perhaps the most authentic and devastating exposure of human sinfulness ever phrased, in Romans 7. And thus we have set before us the major part of the meaning of the Holy Spirit for the problem of sin—God's instrument of deliverance from the grip of sin.

But there is another aspect of the total reality of sin, in some ways far more poignant and perplexing, and strangely bypassed in most classical Christian treatments of the problem. For any serious examination of sin discloses that it lays upon us a burden far heavier than is encompassed even in the stain of sin which must be erased, and the grip of sin which must be broken, and the guilt of sin which must be forgiven. There is also the social consequences of sin—the measureless and endless and irretrievable harm which our sins have disseminated out through the body of humanity, as a pebble dropped in the sea sends its ripples in ever-widening circles until finally every drop in the ocean is affected and every shore touched by its influence. Christ's holiness may purify us of the stain of sin; the power of His Spirit may break the grip of sin upon our lives; God's forgiveness mediated by Him may ease our guilt; all together may prompt us to attempt to overtake the wrong we have done directly to others and to seek their forgiveness. But, what about the wider circle of harm which has gone forth from us through them and is reaching out even now through the common life to touch with blight every one of our fellow-men, and will continue to stain and pervert and curse humankind unto the tenth and hundredth generation? Here, I would urge, is the deepest agony of sin; and, parenthetically, the theological necessity of what we call the "social gospel," not as an incidental corollary to Christian ethics, but as a vital constituent of Christian Faith. What can we do about that?

Very little, indeed, even if our whole life hereafter be given wholly, as it should be, to the redemption of our evil influence, for time and for eternity. But if the Holy Spirit be the ceaseless, tireless activity of Divine holiness and purification at work through all mankind and through all history, may there be easement for our despair, especially if that Holy Spirit so dwell within us that it uses us, yes even us, as agencies for its transforming and redeeming work? Something like that, Dr. Wheeler Robinson suggests in one of the profoundest and most moving passages of his *The Christian Experience of the Holy Spirit*. Even though the thought may seem somewhat speculative, and perhaps at first only imperfectly convincing, let us hear it in his own words:

> "The disclosure of God's essential nature through Christ in the Holy Spirit awakens the faith that our sins are forgiven. . . . Yet there remains the irrevocable fact of sin, for which we are personally responsible, though penitent and forgiven. There is a transformed present; does not the full work of grace also mean a transformed past? It is here that the crowning work of the Holy Spirit must be done. Our own past acquires a new meaning by our changed attitude towards it, wrought by the Holy Spirit within us, and the memory of sin may thus become a means of grace. But this

partial and individual transformation by the Holy Spirit suggests a complete and racial transformation of realized evil in human history by the same Spirit. We often say that a sinful world redeemed by grace is spiritually richer than a sinless world could ever have been. But this is really to say that God is Spirit, and therefore able to transform even the evil that man has done into good. Faith in God means faith in such an ultimate transformation *sub specie aeternatatis,* and it is the present experience of the transforming power of the Holy Spirit which gives to us our partial and individual glimpse of that divine consummation."[6]

This, I would hold, is the final and most exalted and alone satisfying word of Christian faith regarding sin; and it is a word of the Holy Spirit.

[6] Robinson, *op cit.,* p. 212.

CHAPTER SIX

THE HOLY SPIRIT
AND CHRIST

"I believe in the Holy Spirit—and in Jesus Christ, our Lord."

What difference would it make if not simply the words of the creed but Christian thinking were to follow that order?

As a matter of fact, it might be contended that this is the proper order as it was certainly the chronological order in the Christian apprehension of Christ and the Holy Spirit. While some churchmen speak as though the Holy Spirit became known to men for the first time on the Day of Pentecost as the gift of Christ to His Church, we have observed that recognition of the Holy Spirit long antedated the advent of Christ. However sudden and spectacular its coming upon the first disciples, they recognized it as a fresh outpouring of the same Spirit of God which had spoken and acted all through their nation's history; yes, even from the forming of the world. The newness lay, not in the reality of the Holy Spirit itself, but in the vividness and power of its return. Such fresh visitation had been forecast by the prophet Joel,[1] and also, so later reflection added, by Jesus Himself.[2]

[1] Joel 2:23-32; Acts 2:16-21.
[2] John 14:16-17,26; 15:26. Cp. Luke 24:49; Acts 1:4-5.

2.

The contribution of the Holy Spirit to the Christian understanding of man is on the level of human experience, of
immediate and practical relevance for our life, verifiable by
all. The contribution of the Holy Spirit to our thought of
Christ is necessarily more problematic in character since it
concerns our understanding of the inmost being of Jesus
Christ, though not the flights and fancies of abstruse and
pure speculation regarding the inmost relations within the
Godhead with which the classic theologians were preoccupied.

The problem of the interpretation of Jesus Christ has been,
from the outset, a dual one, posed in these two questions:

How are we to think of Christ's relation to God?

How are we to conceive the relation of the divine and
the human in Jesus of Nazareth?

The Church turned its attention to the two aspects of the
problem in that order; it moved to its final answers in two
steps, each marked by two "ecumenical" conferences. The
answers were:

Christ was divine, "of the same substance as the Father."

Jesus of Nazareth was both fully divine and truly
human.

The principal preoccupation of Christian theology for
three centuries was with the first question—to determine
Christ's relation to God. The upshot was the unqualified
affirmation, first at the Council of Nicaea in 325 and then

at the First Council of Constantinople in 381, that Christ
was truly divine, "of the same substance as the Father."

But, what, then, are we to say of *His human life?* Upon
that question, christological thought for the next three centuries was focussed. The reply was formulated by the Council
of Chalcedon in 451; Christ was "perfect in deity and perfect
in humanity" . . . "God truly and man truly" . . . "acknowl-
edged in two natures, without confusion, without change,
without division, without separation . . . not divided or
separated into two persons but one and the same Son and
only begotten God Logos, Lord Jesus Christ." This formula
was made more precise by the Sixth Council of Constantinople in 680 in the declaration that Christ had two wills, a
divine and a human, and two energies fully operative.

That those statements rightly define Christian belief concerning Jesus Christ has never been seriously challenged.
But how are we to understand what they declare? The
baffling question is not "what?" but "how?" It is precisely at
these troublous points that an approach to thought of Christ
by way of the Holy Spirit may offer helpful light. It is a
way of approach which, so far as I am aware, has never or
almost never been explored.

3.

The attempt to think out "how" Christ could have been
both divine and human moved along two alternative lines,
one using the idea of "substance" and the other relying upon
the concept of "will." As the words of the Niceno-Constantinopolitan Creed indicate, during the earlier period when

the aim was to establish the unqualified deity of Christ, the
first alternative was followed and the relation of Christ to
God was defined in terms of "substance." But in the later
period, when the purpose was to vindicate the reality of
Jesus' humanity, the second alternative employing the term
"will" prevailed—a victory of the School of Antioch over the
School of Alexandria. Neither alternative line of explanation
—in terms of "substance" or of "will"—was fully satisfactory
and neither ever succeeded in winning the whole-hearted
assent of the whole Church. "Substance," less to the creedal
centuries than to us but even then, suggests something which
is less than fully personal—a mixture of divine and human
essences which is at far remove from the kinship of two
personal beings so clearly set forth upon the pages of our
Gospels; since the major concern of the earlier centuries was
to assure Christ's deity, His true humanity always tended
to be impugned. And not in the early centuries only. As Dr.
D. M. Baillie has recently written in what is widely regarded
as perhaps the soundest as it is certainly one of the most
illuminating examinations of these issues in recent times:

> "The Church ... was continually haunted by a docetism
> which made His human nature very different from ours
> and indeed largely explained it away as a matter of
> simulation or 'seeming' rather than reality. . . .

> "The cruder forms of docetism were fairly soon left
> behind, but in its more subtle forms the danger con-
> tinued in varying degrees to dog the steps of theology
> right through the ages until modern times."[3]

[3] D. M. Baillie, *God Was in Christ*, pp. 11, 20.

Contrariwise, while the affirmation of a human "will" in Jesus of Nazareth protected the reality of His human life, the assertion that in Him there were two "wills" fully present and operative—one human, the other divine—suggests a monstrosity, neither true man nor yet true God.

If choice must be made between these two alternatives—the employment of "substance" or of "will" to define the identity of Christ with God—the second is to be preferred, as indeed it was by the later creed makers. It has been ably and persuasively restated in our day:

> "We may think of two wills or minds as identical in content while remaining formally distinct. . . . Christ was one with the Father in character, in purpose, in love. It is doubtful whether the union of the Son with the Father can be expressed in higher terms than in terms of harmony of mind and spirit, identity of conscious purpose, complete mutual understanding and fellowship and cooperation, community of values. . . . When we assert that Christ is one with the Father in character and purpose, we have reached a point beyond which we cannot advance except by a leap into the abyss of an abstract and unknowable Absolute."[4]

> "The Form of His Consciousness is human, its content Divine. The whole content of His Being—His thought, feeling and purpose—is also that of God. That is the only 'substance' of a spiritual being, for it is all there is of him at all."[5]

But we do not feel wholly satisfied with that interpretation

[4] D. Miall Edwards, "A Christology in Modern Terms," in *The Lord of Life*, pp. 212 ff.

[5] William Temple in *Foundations*, p. 248.

in terms of the agreement of divine and human wills. The relationship so described is, after all, still an external one —two independent centers of moral purpose acting always in complete harmony. Christian Faith has always felt that the relationship of Jesus to His Father was somehow more intimate, more interior than these terms suggest. Something which the earlier rendering in terms of "substance," with all its failure to recognize the truly personal character of both God and Christ, rightly safeguarded has been lost.

4.

To think of both God and Christ in terms of "spirit" promises to give us a more adequate comprehension and expression of their relationship.

A hint in that direction is furnished us by the most intimate relationship between two human persons. Kinship of ideals, identity of purposes, harmony of wills suggest a relationship of great and mutually enriching intimacy. But marriage in its ideal fulfillment, even friendship at its highest levels, knows a unity which is deeper, richer, more pervasive, an interdependence and mutuality more complete and indissoluble even than that—when two persons, unconsciously, undeliberately, inevitably, think the same thoughts, feel the same emotions, desire the same good as well as will the same end. This is a communion of spirit whereby two persons have become, to all intents and purposes, one.

We draw closer to our goal when we reflect upon our own experience of the indwelling of God's Spirit within our spirits:

"We cannot hope to separate the Spirit of God from the spirit of man, and to make God somehow an 'object' of our consciousness, like other objects. Such controversies as those between the Calvinist and the Arminian as to divine grace and human freedom are not so much settled as superseded; we have caught a deeper glimpse of Christian experience, in its unity. We have learnt to say: 'There is no spiritual power but in God. The well of water, springing up within us, is His Spirit, given at the first, increased from time to time, through the working of this Spirit in the lives and writings of men, and made permanent at last by the appearing of Christ, and our conscious acceptance of Him and His Holy Spirit. . . . God's work all of it, and man's work all of it.'

"The discovery of God is not, then, the discovery of something in a corner of our experience. It is the discovery of Someone Whose presence gathers the whole of our experience into the comprehensiveness of His being, and gives it a new unity."[6]

This fact of Christian experience is expressed classically in Paul's great word, "It is no longer I who live; Christ lives in me." (Galatians 2:20) Had Paul joined this word to the Galatians with his closely parallel word to the Romans (8:9), might he not as well have said: "It is no longer I who live; the Spirit of Christ which is the Spirit of God which is the Holy Spirit lives in me"? This is "the communion of the Holy Spirit" which, in ideal, is to be ours always.

[6] Robinson, *The Christian Experience of the Holy Spirit*, pp. 203-204. Robinson quotes from George Steven, *The Psychology of the Christian Soul*, p. 240.

If this be the truest, most adequate rendering of the realities of consummate Christian experience—the indubitable fact of the experience of the Christian man in whom Christ dwells—how much more appropriately may it be used to suggest the inmost being of Jesus Christ. What is imperfectly true of us, even of the Apostle Paul, was, for Him and in Him, perfectly realized; so that He might have paraphrased Paul's declaration as His own: "I live; yet not I, but the Father lives in me"; or, as the Fourth Gospel puts it: "I and the Father are one." (John 10:30) Quite literally, God dwelt in Him fully, wholly—the Holy Spirit which is the Spirit of God, His Father—as fully and completely as God's Holy Spirit can possess a truly human life.

How could this be? Again, we are led back to a suggestion which has been earlier driven home upon us. What if the Logos which the Fourth Evangelist sets as the prologue to his Gospel, the forerunner of Christ, and which the Church theologians took up and made their central term to interpret the incarnation had been recognized, not as the Word of God or as the pre-existent Christ, but as the Holy Spirit?

> "In the beginning was the Spirit, and the Spirit was with God, and the Spirit was God. . . . All things were made by Him. . . . In Him was life, and the life was the light of men. . . . That was the true light, which lighteth every man that cometh into the world.
>
> "And the Spirit was made flesh, and dwelt among us, full of grace and truth."

As we observed earlier, such a rendering might claim far closer fidelity both to the generally prevailing meaning of

Logos in the thought of the time and to the historic connotation of Spirit throughout Scripture, notably the account of
creation in Genesis 1, but also Paul's glorious portrayal of the
Spirit in Romans 8. Such a rendering would have saved the
mind of the Church of the ages from its exceedingly dubious
speculation regarding the agency of Christ in creation, and
thus have helped to safeguard christology against its most
persistent and debilitating heresy—implicit if not explicit
denial of the true humanity of Jesus.

5.

However, the illumination for our thought cast by reflection upon the relations of the Holy Spirit and Christ is not
unilateral but reciprocal, as is likewise the case when we
examine the relations of the Holy Spirit and man, and the
Holy Spirit and God the Father. Not only does the Holy
Spirit help us to interpret the fact of Christ in terms which
are both credible and true to Christian apprehension. No
less important; Christ defines for us the character of the Holy
Spirit, enabling us to distinguish what is truly "of the Spirit"
from the multitudinous, varied and often fantastic "claims"
to possession by the Holy Spirit or guidance from the Holy
Spirit. As Canon Streeter said:

> "What is this Holy Spirit? It is no other than the
> spirit manifested in the life of Christ. If Christ is our
> portrait of the Father, He is no less our portrait of the
> Holy Ghost."[7]

[7] B. H. Streeter, *The Spirit*, p. 371.

This had been anticipated by Paul in his classic definition: "The Lord is that Spirit." By the same token, only that which is clearly "of the Lord," that is, fully and undeniably akin to the Spirit of Christ, is truly the Holy Spirit.

CHAPTER SEVEN

THE HOLY SPIRIT

AND GOD

"I believe in the Holy Spirit—
and in God the Father Almighty."

What difference would it make if not simply the words of the creed but Christian thinking regarding God were to follow that order? It might be contended that that, also, is the proper order, since it certainly rightly reflects the chronological order in man's apprehension of God; his first awareness is not of God the Father Almighty, Creator of Heaven and earth, but of the immediate and potent presence of Divine Spirit here and now.

Obviously, our thought of the Holy Spirit stands in a different position in its bearing upon our thought of God than in its meaning for any other aspect of Christian belief. For the Holy Spirit is, of course, an aspect or function of God Himself. So to say, the Doctrine of the Holy Spirit is, properly, within the Doctrine of God.

We have noted from our historical review that, with all the differences of apprehension and interpretation, Divine Spirit has signified always and in every context God-near and God-at-work. It has stressed the intimate presence of God and it has stressed the altogether adequate power of God, available in every situation and for every need. These two omnipresent and unfailing characteristics of recognition of Divine Spirit suggest the major contributions of the Holy Spirit to the Christian's thought of God.

2.

The Christian understanding of God is always in danger of distortion or perversion from one or more of three sharply contrasted inadequacies:

1. God may be thought of as an aloof if not impassive Creator, removed from direct involvement in mankind's struggles in history and inaccessible to each man in his personal trials and needs. This inadequacy springs from an extreme or one-sided emphasis upon the transcendence of God. It creeps into Christian thought from non-Christian Deism. In Christian Faith, it is the heresy of exclusive attention to God, the Father Almighty.

2. God may be thought of as impersonal energy or structure, enmeshed within His world but not actively at work upon it and its human inhabitants. This inadequacy results from an exaggerated stress on the immanence of God. It creeps into Christian thought from non-Christian Pantheism. In Christian Faith, it is the heresy of a faulty interpretation of the Holy Spirit.

3. God may be conceived solely in personal terms, in the image of man. This inadequacy results from an uncritical insistence upon the personality of God. It is analogous

to the crude anthropomorphism of primitive religion. In Christian Faith, it sometimes results from exclusive emphasis upon Christ and yields the heresy of Jesuolatry.

3.

Against each of these one-sided distortions, a full-orbed Christian Faith provides adequate safeguards:

1. The first heresy, Christian Deism, is corrected both by emphasis upon the Incarnation—God truly present in the life of Jesus Christ; *and* by recognition of the Holy Spirit —God actively at work throughout the whole of His Creation and intimately available to the soul of every man. But the persistence of this perversion is vividly and tragically illustrated in popular Roman Catholic piety, where God the Father Almighty remains aloof from the toils and frustrations of human experience, impassible (incapable of suffering), while Jesus Christ becomes the intermediary between man and a transcendent inaccessible Deity. Its extreme perversion and *reductio ad absurdum* appears in Mariolatry, where Christ likewise is too pure, too aloof to serve even as point of contact between the worshipper and the Father, and the Virgin Mary takes His place as the effective intermediary between men and both the Father and the Son.

Against this heresy, the Holy Spirit is the altogether adequate and effective safeguard. To quote Dr. Wheeler Robinson once more:

> "The primary value which the Holy Spirit safeguards is the real presence of God in human personality through faith in Christ. If God is really present by His

Holy Spirit in human life, then it is the whole God-head with which we have to do, in all the values of the divine presence. God as Holy Spirit, therefore, may be conceived as present in all His activities, creative, re-demptive and sanctifying. The Holy Spirit in fact repeats within the human life the whole work of God without the life."[1]

2. The second heresy, Christian pantheism—a heresy to which a too exclusive stress upon the Holy Spirit may tempt Christian thought—is decisively corrected by the recognition of Jesus Christ as veritably God-in-human-flesh; and of the Holy Spirit as the Spirit of Christ; that is, by a sound inter-pretation of the Holy Spirit.

3. But, it is with respect to the third heresy—exaggerated or crude anthropomorphism—that the Holy Spirit brings unexpected and needed corrective.

Christian theism finds Personal Purpose or Purposeful Personality to be the most adequate (i.e., least inadequate) way to think of God. The justification of thinking of God in terms of personality is found in the discovery of the presence of Divine Spirit throughout Creation but reaching its climax in man. And the Creative Personal Spirit is given its ethical, holy character as it is defined by the Supreme Person, Jesus Christ. This is another contribution of Paul's great insight which identifies the Spirit of God with the Spirit of Christ. Continuing the quotation from Canon Streeter:

"If Christ is our portrait of the Father, he is no less our portrait of the Holy Ghost. The characteristic ex-pression of the Spirit, as seen in Christ's life, is con-

[1] Robinson, *The Christian Experience of the Holy Spirit*, p. 238.

structive thought and creative effort. Today everyone is crying out for the creative spirit. And this, if only we will see it, is the spirit manifested in the life of Christ."[2]

But even this conception is not altogether adequate or satisfactory. Its inadequacy springs from the inescapable association of the thought of personality or purpose with a specific center of consciousness or will. God tends to be conceived somewhat apart from His Creation rather than present always and altogether throughout His Creation. Not infrequently, this results from thinking of God too exclusively in terms of Christ.

> "The metaphors of 'Fatherhood' and 'Sonship' are so integral to the Christian revelation that, religiously, they can never be displaced; but they remain metaphors. The history of Christian doctrine along the lines of both orthodoxy and heresy shews the tyranny of these metaphors, when they have been pressed into the service of theology and philosophy; so used, they never escape from the perils of anthropomorphism, even whilst they conserve some of its essential truth. The term 'Spirit' is of a different order, not less a metaphor, as all human language must be, but a metaphor drawn from a different sphere, and so corrective of the perils of the others."[3]

The conception of the Holy Spirit enables us to think of that same will and purpose present in human flesh in Jesus Christ as pervasively present throughout all Reality.

[2] B. H. Streeter, *The Spirit*, p. 371 (abbreviated).
[3] Robinson, *op. cit.*, p. 243.

4.

Thus, the Holy Spirit not only enlarges and enriches, but also corrects, our thought of God, leading it into that fullness of apprehension which is suggested for Christian thought, however puzzlingly, by the conviction of the Trinity.

And thus, we are drawn on to recognize both the validity and the value, yes necessity, of the Christian conviction of the Trinity. To that recognition—inevitable copestone of all full-orbed thought of the Holy Spirit—we shall return in our concluding chapter.

But first, we must turn aside to consider some of the troublesome issues which are raised by the relation of the Holy Spirit to the Church.

CHAPTER EIGHT

THE HOLY SPIRIT
AND THE CHURCH

No consideration of the role of the Holy Spirit in Christian faith, however cursory and fragmentary, can conclude without at least brief attention to the relation of the Holy Spirit to the Church. In our own day, there are at least two inescapable imperatives to such attention. The fact that these imperatives arise from powerful voices and forces so to say at opposite extremes of the wide arc of viewpoint regarding the Church within the Church lends added interest as well as importance to such an inquiry.

1. On the one hand, examination of the relation of the Holy Spirit to the Church brings us at once to the heart of the issues which most grievously divide Christians, preventing whatever degree and form of union may be recognized as God's intention for Christ's Church.

One of the great gains of the studies and discussions which have taken place within the developing Ecumenical Movement in recent decades is that they have served to clarify and identify the presently insurmountable divisions among Christians. Contrary to the impression which is widespread especially among laity, the issues on which there is such dissensus among the Churches as to hold them apart are *not* in the great fundamentals of the faith—what Christians affirm concerning God, the World, man, Christ, salvation, eternal life. To be sure, on these matters there are many differences of conviction and they are often deep and sharply contended. But these differences are found *within* Churches, within almost all Churches, and not *between* Churches. They are not the causes of continuing Church disunion. At the Edinburgh Conference of 1937, all these topics of basic theological belief were brought together under a single heading and the Conference prefaced its treatment of them with this unanimous affirmation:

> "We agree on the following statement and recognize that there is in connection with this subject no ground for maintaining division between churches."[1]

Subsequent discussions have confirmed this remarkable declaration.

What, then, are the causes of continuing division? They have been discovered to lie wholly within the Doctrine of the Church, more specifically what the several Churches claim about *themselves,* especially their nature, their ministries, and their authority.

More than that. These same inquiries have revealed that these crucially divisive differences concerning the Church center on what is maintained about the relation of the Holy Spirit to the Church.

Dr. George S. Hendry introduces his admirable brief discussion of this topic with three quotations:

[1] *Faith and Order, Edinburgh 1937*, p. 224.

"Different beliefs about the Church are rooted in different beliefs or unbeliefs about the Holy Spirit."[2]

"Many of our disagreements about the nature of the Church will be further clarified by renewed investigation of the New Testament relationship between the Holy Spirit and Christ, the Holy Spirit and the Word, as well as the Holy Spirit and the Church."[3]

"In our work we have been led to the conclusion that it is of decisive importance for the advance of ecumenical work that the doctrine of the Church be treated in close relation to the doctrine of Christ and to the doctrine of the Holy Spirit."[4]

The last of the three quotations is the latest and most authoritative ecumenical declaration on the issues of Christian division and unity. Dr. Hendry adds: "When we take up the question of the relation between the Holy Spirit and the Church, it is clear that we are entering one of the most controversial areas of current theological discussion in the ecumenical field."[5] We are brought face to face with the crux of the problem of Church union.

2. The other major incentive to inquiry into this theme comes from the "opposite pole," from those dynamic and powerful movements in contemporary Christendom which stand, in considerable measure, outside the ecumenical development and which are widely referred to as "the Sects."

[2] A. R. Vidler, *Christian Belief*, p. 73.
[3] *The Church: Report of a Theological Commission on Faith and Order*, p. 58.
[4] *Faith and Order: The Report of the Third World Conference at Lund, Sweden, August 15-28, 1952*, p. 11.
[5] George S. Hendry, *The Holy Spirit in Christian Theology*, Chapter III, "The Holy Spirit and the Church," p. 53.

It is abundantly clear that the truth of the faith which virtually all of these movements, notwithstanding their diversities and contrasts, claim to have laid hold of, rescuing it from its recent neglect by both Protestantism and Catholicism in their responsible and respectable expressions, and which constitutes the dynamic heart of their message is—the living Reality, Activity and Potency of the Holy Spirit. Thus, in examining the relation of the Holy Spirit to the Church, we are brought face to face with the most baffling and disturbing challenge to conventional Christianity in our day.

The fate of the Holy Spirit at the hands of the theologians and Church officials across the centuries has been summarized in our historical review. It is, on the whole, a pathetic and tragic story:

> The indubitable centrality of the Holy Spirit in the life and message of the Earliest Church.
>
> Its regnancy in the faith and thought of the Apostle Paul.
>
> Its capture and imprisonment by Catholic ecclesiasticism.
>
> Its release and renewal in every epoch of spiritual revival.
>
> Its re-imprisonment by the classic Reformers within the text of Scripture.
>
> Its emancipation with power by the so-called "Radical Reformation," the "Reformation Sects."

Its gradual quiescence into innocuous conventionality
in their later respectability.

Today, its reappearance in familiar excess and wonted
power in the contemporary "sects."

A review of the "biography" of the Holy Spirit through
Christian history discloses that it has been at the heart of
Christian experience and Christian proclamation whenever
they have been vital and dynamic. But the Holy Spirit has
always been troublesome, disturbing because it has seemed
to be unruly, radical, unpredictable. It is always embarrassing
to ecclesiasticism and baffling to ethically-grounded, responsible durable Christian devotion. And so it has been carefully
taken in hand by Church authorities, whether Catholic or
Protestant, and securely tethered in impotence. But—the
Spirit will not long be silenced. When neglected or denied
by the prevailing "churchianity," it unfailingly reappears
to reassert its power, often with excesses and aberrations,
beyond the bounds of conventional Church life.

It is in such historical perspective that we should view the
claims to "recovery of the Holy Spirit" in the "sect" movements of our time.

2.

Dr. Hendry rightly identifies three major alternative interpretations of the relation between the Holy Spirit and the
Church which have appeared in the history of Christian
thought and which are widely argued today.

"Broadly speaking, we can distinguish three views which are taken of this relation: the Roman Catholic view (with which we may associate the very similar Anglo-Catholic view), the view of the Protestant Reformation [or, as we would consider more accurate, the view of Classic Protestantism], and the Spiritualist or Enthusiast view."[6]

Let us examine each of these three alternatives in turn.

i

Official Roman Catholic dogma on the relation of the Church to the Holy Spirit (note the reversal in the order of the two key terms; this is deliberate) is set forth in a sequence of comparatively recent Papal pronouncements dating from the end of the last century. The argument is clear, simple and direct: Christ's work of salvation was not completed during His earthly life; it was essential that it be continued through all subsequent history; for that purpose, the Apostles were commissioned; to enable the Apostles (and their successors) to fulfill that task, the Holy Spirit is given them.

"The Son of God assumed human nature . . . and thus living on earth he taught his doctrine and gave his laws, conversing with men.

"And since it was necessary that his divine mission should be perpetuated to the end of time, he took to

---

[6] Hendry, *op. cit.*, p. 54. It will be noted that the pages which follow draw heavily on Dr. Hendry's excellent exposition.

himself disciples, trained by himself, and made them partakers of his own authority. . . .

"But since it is obviously most in harmony with God's providence that no one should have confided to him a great and important mission unless he were furnished with the means of properly carrying it out, for this reason Christ promised that he would send the Spirit of truth to his disciples to remain with them forever."[7]

Clearly, this teaching hews very close to Scripture, especially the promise of the Spirit in the Fourth Gospel. It seems to provide for the recognition of the Holy Spirit as the living source of illumination and empowerment continuing Christ's work by His followers through all time. The departure of Roman Catholic thought from full acknowledgment of the Holy Spirit is in its limitation of the operation of the Spirit to the "successors of the Apostles" interpreted as the Church hierarchy. Thus, the betrayal of authentic Christian faith is not, in the first instance, in its interpretation of the Holy Spirit but in its dogma of the Church. To be sure, as Dr. Hendry reminds us, "The pope is at pains to resist the inference that these bearers of the apostolic succession have a monopoly of the Holy Spirit. He stresses that the Holy Spirit 'is personally present and divinely active in all the members,' but he adds this qualification that 'in the inferior members [i.e. the laity] he acts also through the ministry of the higher members [i.e. the clergy].' "[8] The contention of many Anglo-Catholic theologians is not substantially different: "The apostolate represents the 'essential ministry' and

[7] Leo XIII, *Satis cognitum*, June 20, 1896, quoted from *The Great Encyclicals of Leo XIII*, pp. 351 ff., 361 f. (cited in Hendry, *op. cit.*, pp. 55, 121).

[8] Hendry, *op. cit.*, p. 59.

this essential ministry is continued in the episcopate, which is thus 'the repository of the commission which Christ gave his apostles.' "[9]

Contemporary Catholic teaching merely codifies and explicates the position to which the official leadership of the Church had been led over the centuries. The development of Mediaeval thought and its consequences for the effective power of the Holy Spirit in the awareness and experience of believers has been well summarized thus:

> "During the Middle Ages, Augustine's doctrine of grace, and of the Holy Spirit as its author, was so submerged by other factors, that all practical interest in the Spirit passed out of the consciousness of the Church. . . . It was held as a theoretical belief that the Holy Spirit acted behind and through the agents and acts of the Church, and it was invoked as the source of the dogma and authority of the hierarchy, but the lower agents occupied the whole field of men's vision and interest, so that the doctrine of the Spirit had no longer any ground in religious experience."[10]

As we have noted in our historical review, it was the Council of Trent in 1545-1563, compelled to meet the challenge of the Protestant Reformation, which advanced the most explicit claims for the direction of its deliberations and decisions by the Holy Spirit, and these claims were pressed to their logical limit in the doctrine of papal infallibility in 1870.

It can be seen that the Catholic position is buttressed by one or more of three independent and complementary lines of argument—biblical, historical, theological:

[9] *Ibid.,* p. 60, quoting *The Apostolic Ministry,* K. E. Kirk, Ed.
[10] T. Rees, *The Holy Spirit in Thought and Experience,* pp. 173-174.

a. *Biblical*. The New Testament, and especially the Gospel of John, specifically promises the Holy Spirit as Christ's gift to His Church.

b. *Historical*. The whole development of the Christian Movement, especially in its struggles with heresy and schism, both substantiates the Church's claim to protection and guidance by the Holy Spirit and vindicates its contention that it is *only* in and through the Church and its officers that the Holy Spirit speaks and acts.

c. *Theological*. "It is obviously most in harmony with God's providence" that those who are charged with responsibility for Christ's mission on earth "should be furnished with the means of properly carrying it out; for this reason Christ promised that he would send the Spirit of truth to his disciples to remain with them forever."[11] This argument rests upon *a priori* reasoning: it was appropriate and therefore necessary and inevitable that God should have provided the Church with the exclusive gift of the Holy Spirit.

ii

As we have earlier had occasion to observe, the debate between Catholicism and classic Protestantism over a true understanding of the Holy Spirit centers on the Spirit's relation respectively to (a) Scripture and (b) Church.

The intention of both of the great Reformers, Luther and Calvin, was to redirect attention from the claims of the Church, not in the first instance to the literal word of Scripture, but to Christ Himself, the Living Word, set before us in

[11] *Encyclical of Leo XIII*, cited above.

the message of the Bible. That is to say, it was thoroughly evangelical. The great work of the Holy Spirit is to point to Christ, to witness to His Lordship, and to confirm in the hearts of believers His judgment and His promises. As Dr. Hendry well contends:

> "The Protestant rejoinder must be that Catholicism fails to recognize the Spirit who indwells as the Spirit who is *Kyrios,* the Spirit whose mission it is to bear witness to Christ. The Spirit who indwells the Roman Catholic Church bears witness to—the Church. . . . In the Protestant understanding the Spirit does truly indwell the Church; only he makes his indwelling presence known, not by inflating the Church with a sense of its own privilege and power, but by directing its attention to its living and exalted Lord and by exposing it to his grace."[12]

So far, so good. Again, we are led along lines which hew close to the thought of the New Testament. If hardly a *full* and adequate interpretation of the Holy Spirit as set forth in the New Testament, this teaching offers a sound and salutary corrective to the false perspective as well as the exaggerated claims of Catholicism.

Unfortunately, this is not the complete or final dogma of the great Reformers and especially of their successors and codifiers. Just as, in earlier centuries, it had been excesses and aberrations defended as inspired by the Holy Spirit and sometimes leading to heresy as well as schism which had furnished "justification" to Catholic theologians for constricting the operations of the Holy Spirit to the word of

[12] Hendry, *op. cit.,* p. 66.

Church authorities, so it was what both Luther and Calvin considered excesses and aberrations among the radical Reformation groups which encouraged the great Reformers, but much more their followers, to invest the word of Scripture which portrays the Word of God with Divine authentication certified by the Holy Spirit. Both the true function of the Holy Spirit in confirming to our hearts the witness of Scripture to God's Word and the illegitimate extension of that function to the divine dictation of the word of Scripture itself are clearly revealed in the familiar and justly famous passage from the First Book of Calvin's Institutes:

> "As God alone is a sufficient witness to himself in his own Word, so also the Word will never gain credit in the hearts of men, till it be confirmed by the internal testimony of the Spirit. . . . For though it win our reverence by its internal majesty, it never seriously affects us till it is sealed by the Spirit in our hearts. Thus, being illuminated by his power, we believe, not on the strength of our own judgment or that of others, that Scripture is from God; we establish it with a certainty superior to human judgment (just as if we actually beheld the presence of God Himself in it) that Scripture came to us, by the ministry of men, from the very mouth of God."[13]

As Dr. Hendry summarizes the upshot of this passage, "The testimony of the Spirit is equivalent to an affidavit that God is the author of Scripture."[14] Nevertheless, Calvin himself did not go on to work out the logical implications of this

[13] *Institutes* I, 7, 4 f.
[14] Hendry, *op. cit.*, p. 76.

view. "He is content to say that the Spirit of God spoke by the mouth of the prophets, and to rest this conviction on the witness of the same Spirit in our hearts."[15]

The development of Calvin's teaching into the full-orbed doctrine of verbal inerrancy of Scripture was the work of the theologians of Protestant Scholasticism. But this extension was not, in principle, novel or peculiar to the Reformation. It had been anticipated in the Roman Catholic view of Scripture.

iii

Earlier we reminded ourselves that the Reformation should never be viewed, as it has been viewed traditionally and is still widely interpreted today, as a three-pronged movement, resulting in the three alternative forms of Protestantism— Lutheran, Calvinist or Reformed, and Anglican or Episcopal (so far as the latter is prepared to accept the designation "Protestant"!) It was a *four*-pronged historic development. To be sure, the fourth phase followed much less clearly defined and coherent lines than the other three. It sprang up in different localities, from unrelated inspirations, and assumed different forms. Indeed, this diversity was inherent in its origins—that it was not due, as were both Lutheranism and Calvinism, to the commanding influence of a single initiator, or, as in the case of Anglicanism, limited to a single locale and culture. Since this fourth branch of the Reformation had its origin in groups which were usually, in their beginnings, quite small and characteristically stood apart from, and

[15] *Ibid.*, p. 78.

were condemned by, the three large branches of the Reformation no less than by Roman Catholicism, they were generally (and disparagingly) designated as "sects." And since they advanced a far more drastic critique of traditional Catholicism and proclaimed a far more demanding return to the pattern of Early Christianity than did Luther or Calvin let alone the English Reformation, they were often labelled "radicals." Accordingly, this fourth phase of the Reformation in its manifold and varied manifestations is known as Radical or Sectarian Protestantism. Properly, it embraces not only the direct descendants of the Anabaptists and Mennonites and Moravians and Brethren, but likewise Congregationalists and Friends; also, two among the half dozen largest Protestant Communions which, though appearing considerably later, are usually not unwilling to be recognized as children of the Radical Reformation, untimely born—Methodism and the Disciples of Christ.

Furthermore, we took note earlier of the fact that Churches within this "sectarian" tradition, by virtue of their phenomenal growth in the Americas, Asia and Africa, now embrace close to half of the constituency of Ecumenical Christianity, far outnumbering any one of the three branches of "traditional" or "classic" Protestantism and nearly equalling their combined memberships.

While the several expressions of "Sectarian" Protestantism differed among themselves in emphases especially cherished by one or another, for example with respect to baptism, they were virtually at one in their radical interpretation of the nature of the Church. This, in turn, was often though not always closely connected with their rediscovery of the Holy Spirit. Indeed, with respect to their basic teaching about God, their distinctive positive doctrine centers precisely upon their interpretation of the Holy Spirit.

> "While Anabaptists [taken as representative of the Radical Reformation] and Protestantism [i.e. Lutherism and Calvinism] were alike opposed to Rome, there was a radical difference between them in their understanding of the Holy Spirit, and, as everyone knows, Luther's opposition to the Anabaptists was scarcely less bitter than his opposition to Rome."[16]

This distinctive teaching is often, mistakenly, defined as an exclusive insistence upon the direct ministry of the Holy Spirit to each individual, without either mediation through the Church or testing by the objective norm of Scripture or Christ. Thus Dr. Hendry: "The emphasis is laid on the immediate, subjective experience of the Spirit in the individual rather than on his appropriation of 'the redemption purchased by Christ'. . . . The dispensation of the Spirit superseded the historical revelation of Christ. . . . The spiritualist individual experiences his own conversion and the resultant spiritual glow rather than Jesus Christ and him crucified; when he bears his testimony, it is to speak of his new-found peace and happiness rather than to confess that Jesus Christ is Lord."[17]

While this criticism unquestionably has point when directed against some of the more extreme, and often obscure and relatively inconsequential, instances of the movement, it comes close to an inexcusable misrepresentation, even travesty, of its major expressions. The latter have been indifferent to neither Scripture and Christ nor Church. On the contrary,

[16] *Ibid.*, p. 68.
[17] *Ibid.*, pp. 68-69.

it is a well-known fact that most forms of "sectarian" Christianity, whether in Reformation times or in the Eighteenth Century or today, have been strongly "biblicist"; often they do not deviate from later Calvinism's assumption of the verbal inerrancy of Scripture. Furthermore, they are often strongly Christo-centric in their piety; their rapid and wide-ranging extension occurred during the Nineteenth Century, the period of most marked Christo-centrism in Christian history, and was partly an expression of the revitalization of faith and life born of a "return to Christ." Even in their view of the relation of the Church to the Holy Spirit, they are widely misunderstood and misrepresented. They firmly oppose ecclesiasticism and what they believe to be unscriptural pretensions for the authority of Church tradition. But they do not sit loose to the Church, especially as the locus in which the Holy Spirit normally operates and by which claimed visitations of the Holy Spirit to the individual are to be checked and held true to the Faith. Usually, they insist that all that is held to be direct guidance from the Holy Spirit to single Christians shall be confirmed or if need be corrected and even negated by the larger wisdom of the Christian community.[18]

The distinctive contention of Radical or Sectarian Protestantism with respect to the Holy Spirit is twofold:

1. That the leading of the Holy Spirit is not confined to the confirmation of the words of Scripture, but guides into "new

[18] For example, among the Friends, through "the sense of the Meeting." Dr. Rufus Jones' charming spiritual autobiography of his youth, *Finding the Trail of Life,* sets forth some delightful illustrations of the restraint upon the misguided "guidance" of the individual through such corporate discipline. Even the "Group Movement" (Moral Rearmament or Buchmanism) which has revived the concept of "divine guidance" in our own day, sometimes in an extravagant form, provides for rigorous discipline upon individual claims by submission to "the Group" which is mandatory upon all members, except possibly the Supreme Leader.

truth" which God desires to reveal to His children in the special and novel circumstances of their contemporary life.

2. That the operation of the Holy Spirit is not limited to the channels and officials of the institutional Church, but comes directly to expectant and contrite spirits in our time as it has through all the ages.

In its second contention, this understanding of the Holy Spirit stands close to Classic Protestantism against the claims of all forms of Catholicism. But, in its first contention, it brings sharp criticism upon the "archaism" of traditional Protestantism, which would limit the Spirit's teaching to the content of the Biblical text. Here, rather than in loyalty to Christ or even reverence for Scripture, is the real battle-ground between the Classical and Radical Reformations. And here, also, lies, for most of us, the special challenge of the widespread revival of radical sectarianism in our day.

3.

We have said that Catholicism, in seeking to substantiate its view of the relation of the Holy Spirit to the Church, makes appeal to one or more of three alternative lines of reasoning—*Biblical, historical, theological*. Each of the other principal interpretations likewise bases its position on one or another of these supports.

It is noteworthy that enlightened Catholicism appears to lean increasingly on the third, the *theological* argument. This is especially true of the ablest exponents of Anglo-Catholic thought. No longer do they attempt to vindicate their own

form of Church-order and authority on *Biblical* evidence, by
discovering it as the only or even the prevailing practice
within the New Testament Church.[19] And while the *historical* consideration to which we shall pass in a moment weighs
heavily with them, they seem to find strongest satisfaction
in the conviction that it was inevitable that God should have
provided for the continuation of Christ's mission through an
authoritative Church and ministry, and that the Holy Spirit
should have been entrusted to them as it also authenticates
them. We noted that the definitive *Encyclical of Leo XIII*,
likewise, while it cites scriptural support for the Catholic
view, seems to place even greater reliance upon a similar
appeal to what is held to be self-evident: "It is obviously most
in harmony with God's providence. . . ."[20]

Of the three types of reasoning, this, the *theological*, is
the least deserving of respect. As we pointed out, it is essentially *a priori*. It attempts to declare what, in the view of those
who hold it, God *must* have done with respect to the creation
and endowment of the Church and the entrustment of the
Holy Spirit to it. But it is obvious that Christians no less
scholarly and no less devout hold directly contrary views of
what "God must have done" and in fact *has* done with
respect to the Church and the Holy Spirit.

Of the three types of argument in support of a "high"
doctrine of the Church (and, by implication, of the relation
of the Holy Spirit to the Church), by all odds the weightiest
is the *historical*. While responsible scholarship in all camps

[19] More than thirty years ago, that great seer and prophet of Anglo-Catholicism,
Bishop Charles Gore, wrote emphatically: "Nothing seems to me more certain
than that the New Testament documents give no decisive indication of the precise
form the ministry was to take." *The Holy Spirit and the Church*, p. 144. Cf. *The
Apostolic Ministry*, a symposium by many of the foremost contemporary Anglo-
Catholic scholars published in 1946.
[20] See above, p. 130.

except orthodox Romanism is now agreed that the New Testament clearly reveals varied practices and patterns in the Earliest Church with respect to Church order, types and designations of ministries, and locus and extent of authority, such scholarship is no less of one mind that, very early, certainly within a century or two, the hierarchical organization of the Church with the differentiation of bishops, priests and laity had established itself almost universally. To those who are persuaded that developments within the Christian Movement which have become well-nigh universal and enduring can hardly have so vindicated themselves contrary to the Divine Intention, this suggests strong support for the episcopal form of Church order. It seems probable that future ecumenical discussions on the doctrine of the Church and the Ministry will pivot increasingly on the degree of weight to be attributed to this unquestioned datum of history.

However, equal support from history can hardly be urged for the Catholic insistence upon the Church's exclusive guardianship of the Holy Spirit. That development proceeded much more slowly and was very much later in establishing itself even within Catholic dogma. And, in this case, the moulding force of factors of ecclesiastical self-interest and self-justification, while clearly present and powerful in the crystallization of exalted claims for the Church and the hierarchy, is more evident, more influential and of much more dubious Divine support. However, the strongest refutation of the Catholic claim regarding the Holy Spirit springs from all that God has taught us about the nature, purpose and operations of His Holy Spirit, not least in the New Testament. If that refutation required additional *historical* vindication, it can be discovered in what the Holy

Spirit has been pleased to accomplish through precisely those persons and movements who have been clearest and most emphatic in rejecting the Catholic claim.

All three alternative interpretations—the Catholic, the Classic Protestant, and the Radical Protestant—would, of course, desire to find their final justification in *Scripture*. Here, as we should expect, there is sharp disagreement as to the teaching and the weight of the evidence.

There can be no question that the *initial* gift of the Holy Spirit, as the New Testament reports it, came to the disciples-in-community, in the events of the Upper Room on the Day of Pentecost.[21] Moreover, prevailingly though by no means exclusively, the presence of the Holy Spirit as the Book of Acts records it was "in the Church", i.e., within the intimate fellowship (*koinoinia*) of Christians. How could it be otherwise since *Acts* is primarily an account of what took place within the Church? But the evidence even of *Acts* can be and often is overpressed. Peter, justifying to the orthodox leaders of the Church at Jerusalem his radical departure from what they considered proper in his association with uncircumcised Gentiles, declares that "The Holy Spirit told me to go with them without hesitation."[22] That is, the Holy Spirit instructed Peter directly *against* the Mother Church of all the Churches.

When Paul appears upon the scene, the first—and perhaps alone sufficient—refutation of the claimed identification of the Holy Spirit with the Church is the unchallengable fact that, while Paul from the outset moved under guidance of the Holy Spirit, its initial gift came to him, *not* within the fellowship of the Church, but in conversation with a single

[21] Acts 2:1-4.
[22] Acts 11:12.

Christian, Ananias.[23] Twice, Paul recounts his *solitary* encounter with the Living Christ upon the Damascus Road;[24] and recall that for Paul in his mature faith the Holy Spirit was virtually identical with the Spirit of Christ. If Paul had conceived that the Holy Spirit as it came to hold a central role in his Christian life was a gift from the Church, or in any sense dependent upon the Church, is it conceivable that, in the countless autobiographical disclosures which stud his letters, he would have failed so much as to reveal, let alone to have affirmed, this fact?

Paul's first encounter with the Church was at Jerusalem; it was marked by conflict; there is no mention of the Holy Spirit![25] Later, Peter, again in dispute with the leaders of the Mother Church at Jerusalem, this time in defense of Paul's ministry not his own, affirms: "God who knows the heart bore witness to them, giving them the Holy Spirit just as he did us; and he made no distinction between us and them."[26] Repeatedly, Paul appeals to his direction by the Holy Spirit: "It has seemed good to the Holy Spirit and to us";[27] but prevailingly the Spirit's guidance comes to him privately not in the Church.

It is not necessary to review again the substance of Paul's teaching regarding the Holy Spirit in his letters. It must suffice to repeat the conclusion to which our earlier examination of this teaching led us:

> ". . . the major emphasis of the Letters of the Imprisonment as of their predecessors is not upon the role of the Spirit in the Church but of its action upon in-

[23] Acts 9:17.
[24] Acts 22:4-16; 26:9-18.
[25] Acts 9:26-30.
[26] Acts 15:8-9.
[27] Acts 15:28. Cp. Acts 16:6,7.

dividuals. Take Ephesians, often held to be the Charter of Paul's doctrine of the Church, for illustration. 'We have access by one Spirit unto the Father.' (2:18) Christians are to be 'renewed in the spirit of their minds.' (4:23) Part of their equipment for spiritual combat is to be 'the sword of the Spirit which is the word of God.' (6:17) . . . In the reading of Paul's climactic thought of the Spirit as wholly or principally a possession of the Church, it appears as though we again confront a familiar trick of interpretation—reading back into earlier teaching views which have become axiomatic for the later interpreters."

In the greatest Pauline passages which deal most directly, most creatively—and definitively—with the Christian Movement (I Corinthians 12, Ephesians 4) the Spirit plays a large part. But its gifts are primarily to individuals: "To each is given the manifestation of the Spirit for the common good. . . . All these are inspired by one and the same Spirit."[28] And, by virtue of participation in this one Spirit, Christians are knit into the unity of the one Body, "eager to maintain the unity of the Spirit in the bond of peace. There is one body and one Spirit."[29] So the Spirit is the animating principle of the community of Christians as of the individual Christian. But the Spirit is not linked explicitly with the Church but with the Body of Christ. (Only in Colossians, of doubtful Pauline authorship, is the "body" spoken of as the "Church.") For Paul the Body of Christ was a very different reality from the Church, either the disparate Christian congregations of his day or the massive ecclesiastical structures of today, although

[28] I Corinthians 12:7-11.
[29] Ephesians 4:3-4.

these "Churches" fulfill their true destiny only as they participate in the Body of Christ. It is the Spirit which bestows unity upon the Church, not the Church which bestows the Spirit upon men.

Even in Ephesians, Paul's final emphasis falls always upon the direct gift of the Spirit, "that he may grant you to be strengthened with might through his Spirit in the inner man . . . to him be glory in the church." "Be filled with the Spirit."[30]

4.

Each of the three rival interpretations of the relation of the Holy Spirit to the Church embraces true and indispensable insights, as we would expect.

It is *the Bible* which not only introduces us to the age-long pilgrimage of conviction regarding the Holy Spirit reaching its fulfillment in the identification of the Holy Spirit as the Spirit of Christ. It is the Bible which alone sets before us the "mind of Christ," and since the Holy Spirit which continues Christ's work *is* the living Spirit of Christ, only through the Bible can we "test the spirits" to make certain that what is claimed to be the Holy Spirit is really so because it is in unmistakable and essential continuity with the spirit of Jesus of Nazareth.

For most of us, first awareness of the Holy Spirit comes through *the Church.* And the wisdom of the Church born of long and stern experience supplies a further necessary safeguard against irresponsible or misguided mis-interpretations of the Spirit's leading and action today.

[30] Ephesians 3:16,21; 5:18.

The issue between the Catholic and the Protestant (whether Classic or Radical) views of the Holy Spirit is, basically, the issue between *Order* and *Freedom*. Order and Freedom, each with its peculiar and inescapable perils. Order, with its perils of rigidity, sterility, sacerdotalism and authoritarianism. Freedom with its perils of individualism, irresponsibility and caprice.

The issue between Catholicism or Classic Protestantism, on the one hand, and Radical Protestantism, on the other, is, largely, the issue between *Tradition* and *Creativity,* each likewise with its own peculiar and inescapable perils.

In more familiar and specifically religious terms, the issue is between the *"priestly"* and the *"prophetic."*

> "For has not priestly religion ever relied more upon the static and the traditional and the ordered than upon the dynamic and the novel and the free? . . . Without a framework of Law and Liturgy religion can easily disintegrate into incoherence and extravagance. Yet it is equally true that unless priestly forms be constantly polarized by the fresh and vital religion of the Spirit, they become hard and sterile."[31]

No one who has studied the history of institutions, not least in Christianity, will doubt that the values of Order and Tradition will find adequate guardians in the Church, whose every instinct is for their preservation. This is not the special task of the Holy Spirit nor its distinctive function. The great need of the Church is for precisely those gifts which can come to it only through the Holy Spirit in its creative and prophetic freedom.

[31] F. W. Dillistone, *The Holy Spirit in the Life of Today,* p. 25.

And so the final emphasis must be given to the gift of the Holy Spirit to each eager and expectant spirit, confirming to it the truths of Scripture, sanctifying it within the Body of Christ, and leading it forth to new duties and upon new discoveries under the power of the Spirit.

NOTE TO PART THREE

After this book was in page-proof, Dr. George S. Hendry's recently published *The Gospel of the Incarnation* came to hand. At a number of points, it adds valuable insights to his exposition of *The Holy Spirit in Christian Theology,* especially in its concluding chapter on "The Extension of the Incarnation" and carries the line of thought developed above one important step farther: "The Christ who was incarnate continues himself in the mission and work of the Holy Spirit. The Holy Spirit is Christ's gift to the church, but never the possession of the church. . . . The extension of the incarnation then must be defined as the presence of the Spirit in the church; for the presence of the Spirit is the presence of Christ." (p. 159)

PART FOUR

CONCLUSION

CHAPTER IX   *The Spirit and the Trinity*

THE SPIRIT

AND THE TRINITY

We suggested at the outset of our inquiry that, of all the beliefs of Christian Faith, the most mysterious and the most mystifying to the ordinary Christian is the Trinity. How frequently and spontaneously we speak of "the mystery of the Trinity"! Mysterious not in the right and desirable sense that it serves to remind us of the greatness of God and the manifoldness of His operations, and so to enlarge and enrich our thought of God, but mysterious in the undesirable sense that it baffles and confuses us in trying to think of God worthily. If the typical layman might follow the candid deacon in confessing that, to him, the Holy Spirit is "a vague, oblong blur," not only he but also his minister might respond to mention of the Trinity by declaring that, for him also, the Trinity is a "vague, oblong (or triangular) blur."

In the same fashion, we tend to think of the doctrine of the Trinity as, not only the most obscure and mystifying but also perhaps the most abstruse and speculative of all Christian beliefs.

It is important to recognize at once that the Trinity is, in the first instance, not a dogma of theology at all but a datum of experience; we need to hold fast to that recognition through all our discussion. Historically the TRINITY OF EXPERIENCE long antedated the TRINITY OF DOGMA. In Canon Hodgson's striking epigram: "Christianity began as a trinitarian religion with a unitarian theology."[1]

We have earlier reminded ourselves that the three-fold designation of God as Father, Son, and Holy Spirit is present within the New Testament in two crucial passages of immense influence upon Early Christianity—the Great Commission and Baptismal Formula attributed to the Risen Christ which concludes the Gospel of Matthew (28:19) *and* the Great Benediction which concludes Paul's Second Letter to the Corinthians (13:14)—and that these two "Trinitarian" phrases worked their way into the heart of Christian thinking through frequent repetition in the worship of the Christian Churches, worship which sought to voice not what theologians presumed to be true of the Being of God but what ordinary Christians knew to be true of their experience of God. Likewise, that the three-fold distinction was a constitutive element of Paul's most creative and central teaching, as in Romans 8, and of the Fourth Gospel in the crucial passage which places on the lips of Jesus the promise of the Counselor, the Spirit of truth, whom the Father will send in His name and who will bear witness to Him and guide His followers into all the truth. (John 14:15-26; 15:26-27; 16:7-15) These great passages in both Paul and John are, again, declarations of experience, of what was already most assuredly known to be fact in the life of the First-century Christian Church.[2]

---

[1] Leonard Hodgson, *The Doctrine of the Trinity,* p. 103.
[2] I John 5:7 ("There are three that bear record in heaven, the Father, the Word, and the Holy Ghost: and these three are one.") appears in no early manuscript and is rejected by the most competent New Testament scholars as a late addition. See *The Interpreter's Bible,* Vol. 12, p. 293.

Whatever we make of the TRINITY OF DOGMA, the TRINITY OF EXPERIENCE remains. Indeed, the crucial question in all speculative thought about the Trinity is precisely this: whether it is legitimate, indeed necessary, to recognize as true of the inmost reality of the Divine Being distinctions which are indisputably real within our experience of the Divine Being. It has been well said:

> "The story of the Trinity in ecclesiastical history is the story of the transition from the Trinity of experience, in which God is self-revealed as the Father or Creator and Legislator, the Son or Redeemer, and the Spirit or sanctifier, to the Trinity of dogma, in which the threefold self-disclosure of God is but the reflexion, as it were, of a threefold distinction within the Divine Nature itself."[3]

The Doctrine of the Trinity, then, is not basically an attempt to foist upon Christian credulity an unintelligible and incredible speculation regarding Ultimate Reality; it is the effort to discover what must be true of Ultimate Reality because of what our experience of that Reality tells us. Affirmation of the Trinity and *some* attempt to explain it are an inevitable and inescapable corollary of Christian certitude.

2.

The next fact to be noted, as with the companion belief in the Holy Spirit, is that the idea of the three-fold character of God or a three-fold distinction within the Divine Being is by no means peculiar to Christianity. On the contrary, it

[3] W.Fulton, article "Trinity," *H.E.R.E.*, Vol XII, p. 459.

is an element widely present in advanced religious thought. Egyptian religion worshipped Osiris, Isis and Horus, and spoke of them as Father, Mother and Son. The Neo-Platonism of Plotinus recognized three elements within the Deity—the Good, Intelligence, and the World-Soul. Contemporary Hinduism has Brahma, Siva and Vishnu as principal deities within its pantheon.

Some years ago, in the course of a journey around the world, my wife and I had the privilege of spending a week as houseguests of the ablest and most influential of the Indian Maharajas, at that time Chancellor of the Chamber of Princes, more recently the first of the Maharajas to be trusted with official appointment by the new democratic government of India as a member of the Indian delegation in the United Nations and Chairman of its Finance Committee. On the first day of our visit, as we were going into lunch, our host paused in the hallway to call our attention to a plaque hanging there, bearing a very striking relief—a black ebony head, showing three faces. The Maharaja explained: "That is a representation of our Hindu Deity. But, unlike your Christian Deity, we do not believe in three Gods, but in a single God with three faces." Then, pointing to the first face, looking out toward the right—an aloof, austere, mysterious countenance—he said: "That is Brahma, the Ultimate Reality." Next, pointing to the second face which stared the onlooker directly in the eyes—a grotesque, distorted, horrific countenance—he went on: "The second face is that of Siva, the Destroyer; for we believe that the powers of destruction no less than the power of creation are within God. The third face [a gentle, reflective, gracious, remote countenance turned away from the beholder toward the left] is Vishnu, the Restorer." It was not opportune, in the first hour of one's visit, to correct him by explaining that his description of the Hindu Deity was a very accurate description of the Christian Deity—not "three Gods but one God with three faces." Nor would it have been courteous to go on to point out that, in the contrast between the second face of the Hindu God—the horrible Siva, with whose worship are associated the worst excesses of cruelty and sensuality of Hinduism—*and* the Second Person of the Christian God— the face of Jesus Christ—is to be found the heart of the conflict of Hinduism and Christianity.

Belief in a triune God is not a distinctively Christian conviction. The distinctive and determinative feature of the Christian Trinity is, precisely, the Incarnation, the definition of the character of God by Jesus Christ.

3.

What, if any, light may the history of Christian thought about the Trinity yield for our present-day understanding of it?

We have already traversed the steps preparatory to the formulation of the doctrine of the Trinity, in the recognition of the Holy Spirit as truly and fully divine, parallel and equal to the Father and the Son.

The earliest attempt at a definitive formulation of the Trinity was the work of that remarkable trinity of eastern theologians known as the Cappadocian Fathers—Basil, his brother Gregory of Nyssa, and their friend and colleague

Gregory of Nazianzus. They begin, rightly, with an honest and humble confession of the incomprehensibility of the Divine Nature and the limitations of human speculation. Gregory Nazianzus declares:

> "It is difficult to conceive God but to define Him in words is an impossibility. . . . In my opinion it is impossible to express Him, and yet more impossible to conceive Him . . . and this, not merely to the utterly careless and ignorant, but even to those who are highly exalted and who love God, and in like manner to every created nature."[4]

Despite this forthright recognition of the impossibility of the attempt, Basil, as a good speculative theologian, cheerfully goes on to interpret the relations of Father, Son and Holy Spirit within the Godhead in terms of the then accepted discrimination of substance from hypostasis (in Greek *ousia* and *hypostasis,* in Latin *substantia* and *persona,* in our usual English translation *substance* and *person*) and explains the Trinity as affirming one *ousia* or *substantia* or "substance" or "nature" in three *hypostases* or *personae* or "persons." Basil writes his brother Gregory of Nyssa:

> "Many, not distinguishing in theology the common substance from the hypostases, fall into the same fancies and imagine that it makes no difference whether substance (*ousia*) or hypostasis be spoken of [*ousia* and *hypostasis* had been used as synonyms as recently as the Council of Nicaea in 325]. Whence it has pleased some to admit without examination that if one substance

---

[4] Gregory Nazianzus, *Nicene and Post-Nicene Fathers,* Second Series, Vol. VII, p. 289, Oratio xxviii, iv.

then also one hypostasis should be affirmed. And on the other hand those who accept three hypostases think themselves compelled to confess an equal number of substances. I have therefore, that you may not fall into a similar error, written you a brief discourse concerning the matter. This then, to put it briefly, is the meaning of the words: Some nouns which are used to cover many and various objects have a more general sense like man (*anthropos*). When we employ this word we designate the common nature (*phusis*) not some particular man to whom the name especially belongs."

Basil then continues:

"For Peter is no more man than Andrew or John or James. Hence, as the word embraces all that are included under the same name, there is need of some mark of distinction by which we may recognize not man in general but Peter or John. There are other nouns which stand for a particular object and denote not the other nature but a separate thing having nothing in common, so far as its individuality goes, with others of the same kind, like Paul or Timothy. . . . Thus when two or more are taken together, such as Paul and Silvanus and Timothy, and inquiry is made concerning their substance, we do not use one word for the substance of Paul, another for that of Silvanus, and another for that of Timothy. . . . If then you transfer to theology the distinction you have drawn in human affairs between substance and hypostasis you will not go wrong."[5]

[5] Basil, *Epistle 38*, to his brother Gregory of Nyssa.

This statement is of the utmost importance not only because of its great historic influence, but also because, in its last sentence, it sets forth frankly the method most frequently employed in all subsequent trinitarian speculation: "to transfer to theology the distinctions drawn in human affairs." Note that while the Cappadocians' writings often sound like the most abstruse speculation, they are really unashamedly anthropomorphic—interpreting the Divine Nature by analogies drawn from human nature.

How, then, in the view of the Cappadocian theologians, are the three "persons" of the Godhead different from each other? Is one to be thought of as Creator, another as Redeemer and the third as Sanctifier? Not at all; all three "persons" function in all three Divine activities. Rather, the Father is unbegotten while the Son is eternally begotten; the Father does not proceed while the Holy Spirit eternally proceeds. The differentiation is no longer, as it was for Paul and John and the Early Church, a difference in the operation of the Divine Being in His creation and upon human life testified by observation and experience, but a description of distinctions within the Godhead for which there is no definable basis, and perhaps can be no basis, within our assured knowledge of God. The TRINITY OF SPECULATION has triumphed over the TRINITY OF EXPERIENCE. And the resulting conception verges precariously toward tritheism. This conception was formally declared by the *Eastern* Bishops and Doctors at an assemblage at Constantinople in 382 (not to be confused with the "ecumenical" Council of Constantinople in the preceding year):

"This is the faith which ought to be sufficient for you, for us, for all who wrest not the word of the true faith;

for it is the ancient faith; it is the faith of our Baptism; it is the faith that teaches us to believe in the name of the Father, of the Son, and of the Holy Ghost. According to this faith there is one Godhead, Power and Being of the Father and of the Son and of the Holy Ghost; the dignity being equal, and the majesty being equal in three perfect hypostases, i.e. three perfect persons."[6]

In the meantime, reflection regarding the Trinity in Western Christendom had moved along somewhat different lines. Here, the determinative mind was that of the great Augustine. It must always be borne in mind that Augustine, like the Western theologians generally, was passionately concerned to safeguard the unity of God in men's thought of Him. Therefore, with him the stress falls on the divine unity while recognizing the three-fold expression of that unity, just as the Eastern theologians generally are most interested in elaborating the distinctions within the Godhead while formally affirming the unity. Furthermore, Augustine, making earnest with the limitations of human thought, was profoundly dissatisfied with his own efforts to conceive and explain the distinctions within the Godhead, while the Eastern writers, despite their pious professions of ignorance, appear to believe that they have achieved precise and indisputable knowledge of the inmost character of the Godhead. Augustine summarizes his definition of the Trinity near the beginning of his lengthy and weighty treatise *On the Trinity:*

"The Father, and the Son, and the Holy Spirit intimate a divine unity of one and the same substance in an indivisible equality; and therefore they are not three Gods, but one God: although the Father hath begotten

[6] Statement of the Eastern Bishops and Doctors, Constantinople, A.D. 382.

the Son, and so he who is the Father is not the Son;
and the Son is begotten by the Father, and so he who
is the Son is not the Father; and the Holy Spirit is
neither the Father nor the Son, but only the Spirit of
the Father and of the Son, himself also co-equal with
the Father and the Son, and pertaining to the unity of
the Trinity. Yet not that this Trinity was born of the
Virgin Mary, and crucified under Pontius Pilate, and
buried, and rose again the third day, and ascended into
heaven, but only the Son. Nor, again, that this Trinity
descended in the form of a dove upon Jesus when he
was baptized; nor that, on the day of Pentecost, after
the ascension of the Lord, when 'There came a sound
from heaven as of a rushing wind,' the same Trinity 'sat
upon each of them with cloven tongues like as of fire,'
but only the Holy Spirit. Nor yet that this Trinity said
from heaven, 'Thou art my Son,' whether when he was
baptized by John, or when the three disciples were with
him in the mount, or when the voice sounded, saying, 'I
have both glorified it and will glorify it again'; but
that it was a word of the Father only, spoken to the
Son; although the Father, and the Son, and the Holy
Spirit, as they are indivisible, so work indivisibly.

"This is also my faith, since it is the Catholic faith."[7]

Thus far, it will be noted, Augustine is merely recognizing
the three-fold operation of the one God on the plane of
human experience. How, then, does Augustine explain the
distinction of Father, Son and Spirit within the Godhead?
He discovers the most helpful suggestions, not as the Cappadocians had, in the analogy of the relations of individual

[7] St. Augustine, *On the Trinity*, I. iv, English translation (Edinburgh, 1873), p. 7.

men to each other, but principally in analogies drawn from the inmost self-consciousness of every man. At different places, Augustine elaborates three alternative analogies which are not altogether mutually consistent or readily reconciled. The Trinity may be likened to:

1. Memory, Understanding and Will—three faculties of one and the same person.

2. Mind, self-knowledge, self-love—also, three aspects of the same individual.

3. The Lover, the Beloved, Love—obviously not three faculties or aspects of a single self-consciousness, but rather of the relations of separate beings. As with the Cappadocians, this third explanation tends strongly toward tritheism: its more serious inadequacy is that the "Third Person," love, is hardly more than a relationship.

The early speculation, both Eastern and Western, found its definitive and official formulation in the so-called Athanasian Creed:

"The Catholic Faith is this: that we worship one God in Trinity, and Trinity in Unity, neither confounding the Persons nor dividing the Substance.

"For there is one Person of the Father, another of the Son, and another of the Holy Ghost; but the Godhead of the Father, of the Son, and of the Holy Ghost is all one—the glory equal, the majesty co-eternal.

"Such as the Father is, such is the Son and such is the Holy Ghost: the Father uncreate, the Son uncreate, and the Holy Ghost uncreate; the Father incomprehensible, the Son incomprehensible, and the Holy Ghost incomprehensible; the Father eternal, the Son eternal, and the Holy Ghost eternal;

"And yet they are not three eternals, but one eternal; as also there are not three incomprehensibles nor three uncreated, but one uncreated and one incomprehensible.

"So likewise the Father is almighty, the Son almighty, and the Holy Ghost almighty; and yet they are not three almighties, but one almighty. So the Father is God, the Son is God, and the Holy Ghost is God; and yet they are not three Gods but one God; so likewise the Father is Lord, the Son Lord, and the Holy Ghost Lord; and yet not three Lords but one Lord.

"For like as we are compelled by the Christian verity to acknowledge every Person by himself to be God and Lord, so are we forbidden by the Catholic religion to say, there be three Gods or three Lords.

"The Father is made of none, neither created nor begotten;

"The Son is of the Father alone, neither made nor created, but begotten;

"The Holy Ghost is of the Father and of the Son, neither made nor created nor begotten, but proceeding;

"So there is one Father, not three Fathers; one Son, not three Sons; one Holy Ghost, not three Holy Ghosts.
"And in this Trinity none is afore or after other, none

is greater or less than another; but the whole three Persons are co-eternal together and co-equal.

"So that in all things, as is aforesaid: Unity in Trinity, and the Trinity in unity, is to be worshipped."

"He therefore that will be saved must thus think of the Trinity."[8]

In summary, classic Christian thought, making its beginning in the indubitable three-fold experience of God as testified by the New Testament, is at one in holding that this TRINITY OF EXPERIENCE must be a reflection (mirror) of the inner nature of the Divine Being, of an ONTOLOGICAL TRINITY. And it is also at one in seeking an understanding of *how* this can be by positing in the Godhead distinctions discovered within human experience, that is by the method of frank anthropomorphism. Not only did the TRINITY OF EXPERIENCE give birth to the TRINITY OF SPECULATION. The TRINITY OF SPECULATON builds upon human experience. Not however— and just here is the dubious point of departure from sound procedure—upon men's experience of God but their experience of themselves, that is by the method of anthropomorphism. It does so along two alternative lines:

1. Starting with the three Persons of the Deity and the problem of how the three Persons can be one God, it studies the relations of human persons to each other, and finds in them a suggestion of the relations of the Divine Persons within the Godhead. (The Cappadocian Fathers and the Eastern Church generally)

2. Starting with the unity of God and the problem of how the one God can be conceived as three "persons," it

[8] The Athanasian Creed.

examines the working of the human soul at its highest, and pictures the inmost Being of God as analogous—on the assumption that man is truly made in the image of God. (Augustine characteristically and the Western Church prevailingly)

4.

Space does not permit us to follow the tortuous course of trinitarian speculation through succeeding centuries. Nor is it necessary to do so. For—and this fact is of the highest interest—though there are ingenious and sometimes suggestive elaborations and modifications in details, all interpretations move along the same two alternative lines. There is no novelty in principle of interpretation.

This is so even of the modern period. By universal acknowledgment, Friedrich Schleiermacher was the "Father of Modern Theology." True to his central emphasis upon the witness of Christian experience, he sought to recall thought of the TRINITY to its starting-point, to replace the TRINITY OF SPECULATION by the original TRINITY OF EXPERIENCE. As the late President McGiffert summarized Schleiermacher's position with characteristic succinctness: "The dogma of the Trinity, he treated not as a statement of eternal distinctions within the Godhead but simply as an indication of the various ways in which God relates himself to the experience of Christians."[9] Schleiermacher was loyal to Church tradition in regarding "the Doctrine of the Trinity . . . as the coping-stone of Christian doctrine." But he brought severe strictures

[9] A. C. McGiffert, *The Rise of Modern Religious Ideas*, p. 289.

against the orthodox formulation of the Trinity on the ground that it could not "be regarded as an immediate or even a necessary combination of utterances concerning the Christian self-consciousness." On the contrary, "the assumption of an eternal distinction in the Supreme Being is not an utterance concerning the religious consciousness, for there it never could emerge." Therefore, "a trinity in God from general conceptions or *a priori* . . . could find no place in a Christian Dogmatic." "We have only to do with the God-consciousness given in our self-consciousness along with our consciousness of the world; hence we have no formula for the being of God in Himself as distinct from the being of God in the world."[10]

But the penchant for speculation will not down. On the contrary, the speculative interpretation of the Trinity has received enormous impetus, and its most elaborate expositions since the Cappadocian Fathers, in the past century. These expositions have moved in two sharply contrasted directions.

Most widely influential have been Hegel and his followers. Indeed, Hegel regarded the Trinity as the central doctrine of Christianity. He contended that Christianity's greatness and its finality lay precisely in its concept of a triune God. He expounded the ontological reality of the Trinity, as he did every other aspect of reality and every event of man's corporate and personal history, in terms of the human self-consciousness as he conceived it—a triadic movement of self-expression and self-fulfillment through the three steps of Thesis, Antithesis and Synthesis. Indeed, God he defined as the Absolute Experience. The Father is the ultimate principle of the Godhead, the thesis of the Divine dialectic, existing in

[10] Friedrich Schleiermacher, *The Christian Faith,* pp. 739-748.

and for Himself from all eternity. The Son is the principle of differentiation or self-expression in the Godhead, separating Himself from the Father in the antithesis of creation, and returning to the Father in the higher synthesis of redemption. It is through the Holy Spirit that Father and Son recognize their unity, and God comes to His full self-consciousness as Spirit.[11] (There are obvious points of contact here with Augustine's third suggestion of the Trinity as the Lover, the Beloved, and Love; though also important differences.)

An even more novel and original interpretation of the Trinity in recent years is the expression, in terms of the inner Being of the Godhead, of one of the passionate enthusiasms of the time—the social emphasis. The argument runs: Since all true experience is necessarily social, we must conceive of the Godhead as a society of persons in relations of mutuality with each other.[12] Here, again, the details of the theory and its justification are modern, but the principle is the same as that which guided the Cappadocian Fathers.

5.

In our own day, in contemporary theology, there have been three reinterpretations of the Trinity of more than usual originality and power.

1. One, as might be anticipated, comes from the mind of Karl Barth. For, to the astonishment of many, Barth's the-

---

[11] G. W. F. Hegel, *Philosophy of Religion* (Eng. Trans.), Vol. II, pp. 327 ff. Cp. H. R. Mackintosh, *Types of Modern Theology*, pp. 101 ff.

[12] Cp., for example, A. C. McGiffert, *The Rise of Modern Religious Ideas*, pp. 275-276. A persuasive interpretation along similar lines was developed by the great prophet of social Christianity, Walter Rauschenbusch, *A Theology for the Social Gospel.*

ology proves to be thoroughly and insistently trinitarian. He declares:[13] "We begin the doctrine of revelation with the doctrine of the Triune God. God Himself in unimpaired unity yet also in unimpaired difference is Revealer, Revealed, Revealedness." . . . "One in three of His own modes of existence, which consist in their mutual relationships—Father, Son and Holy Spirit." Once again, the phrases are reminiscent of Augustine. Like Augustine, Barth never tires of categorical insistence upon the unity of God. "Not three divine 'I's,' but thrice of the one divine I." But he goes on to affirm with equal emphasis: "Anti-trinitarianism falls into the dilemma of denying either the revelation of God or the unity of God." He continues: "We prefer to say, the three 'modes of being' in God, rather than three 'persons.'" This "means that the one God, i.e., the one Lord, the one personal God is what He is not in one mode only, but . . . in the mode of the Father, in the mode of the Son, in the mode of the Holy Spirit." And Barth adds: "The ancient concept of Person . . . . has today become obsolete."

2. In seeming direct contradiction, Canon Leonard Hodgson insists upon the soundness of the classic formula of "three Persons," and seeks to make it intelligible and convincing through an interesting analysis of the nature of unity.[14] He reminds us, as we have already noted, that "Christianity began as a trinitarian religion with a unitarian theology"; that is to say, the problem with which we must wrestle is not how to believe in a triune conception of God, but how to interpret theologically a trinitarian experience of God. The Christian dilemma has always been unitarianism vs. tri-

[13] *The Doctrine of the Word of God*, Vol. I, Part I, pp. 339, 400, 403, 404, 407, 413, 420.
[14] *The Doctrine of the Trinity*, esp. p. 108.

theism. Christian Faith, in fidelity to its knowledge of God in experience, desires to declare a three-fold Deity, but can it succeed in doing so without sacrificing the unity of God? The concept of unity, he holds, may be used in two contrasted senses. There is mathematical unity involving the absence of multiplicity. But there is also organic unity, in which multiplicity is embraced within an "internally constitutive unity." "This world is the world wherein the ultimate unities of reality are made known to us not in their unity but in their multiplicity." In this recognition, it is possible to conceive of three Persons in one God. As Professor D. M. Baillie rightly suggests, Hodgson's interpretation which is representative of contemporary Anglicanism tends toward "tritheism," as Barth's, so influential upon contemporary Reformed Theology, inclines toward "modalism."[15]

3. Much the most original and suggestive reinterpretation of the Trinity in these latter years has come, however, not from the speculations of a theologian, but from the testimony of a layman, or rather a laywoman. Mrs. Dorothy Sayers' *The Mind of the Maker* is the most brilliant and stimulating work of lay theology in our day, as well as one of the boldest efforts to comprehend the Christian affirmation of the Trinity ever penned.

Mrs. Sayers draws the materials for her effort altogether from the data of creative originality as she knows it in her own experience as writer, and as she discovers it in the creative work of others—writers, artists, etc., and as it is verified in the appreciation of artistic creation by those who rightly comprehend what is offered them.

The creative artist begins with an "Idea" in the mind.

[15] *God Was in Christ*, "Two Trends of Trinitarian Thought," pp. 133 ff.

This *must,* by its own inner logic, body itself forth into the world in a ceative Act ("Energy"). But this is not the conclusion of the matter. That which the creator has envisioned, and has given forth, must itself *act* to communicate the "Idea" and the "Energy" to reader or beholder. It even returns to the artist to bring added understanding of his own creative Idea ("Power") and thus to complete the full cycle of creation.[16] Something of this three-step process is experienced by the reader or beholder:

"This threefoldness in the reader's mind corresponds to the threefoldness of the work (Book-as-Thought, Book-as-Written, Book-as-Read), and that again to the original threefoldness in the mind of the writer (Idea, Energy, Power). It is bound to be so, because that is the structure of the creative mind. When, therefore, we consider Trinitarian doctrine about the universal Creator, this is what we are driving at. We are arguing on the analogy of something perfectly familiar to our experience. The implication is that we find the threefold structure in ourselves (who are the-Book-as-Read) because that is the actual structure of the universe (which is the-Book-as-Written), and that it is in the universe because it is in God's Idea about the universe (the-Book-as-Thought). Further, that this structure is in God's Idea because it is the structure of God's mind.

"This is what the doctrine means; whether it is true or mistaken is another matter, but this is the Idea that is put forward for our response. There is nothing mytho-

[16] From *The Mind of the Maker,* copyright 1941 by Dorothy L. Sayers, pp. 40-41.

logical about Christian Trinitarian doctrine: it is analogical."[17]

Let us hear her own summary of her experience as creative artist, and its implications, as she conceives them, for our thought of the Ground of all creation, the Creator God:

"I find in myself a certain pattern which I acknowledge as the law of my true nature, and which corresponds to experience in such a manner that, while my behavior conforms to the pattern, I can interpret experience in power. I find, further, that the same pattern inheres in my work as in myself; and I also find that theologians attribute to God Himself precisely that pattern of being which I find in my work and in me.

"If you ask me what is this pattern which I recognize as the true law of my nature, I can suggest only that it is the pattern of the creative mind—an eternal Idea, manifested in material form by an unresting Energy, with an outpouring of Power that at once inspires, judges, and communicates the work; all these three being one and the same in the mind and one and the same in the work. And this, I observe, is the pattern laid down by the theologians as the pattern of the being of God.

"If all this is true, then the mind of the maker and the Mind of the Maker are formed on the same pattern, and all their works are made in their own image."[18]

Here, again, is unmistakable reminiscence of Augustine, and also perhaps of Hegel. This is abstruse speculation made intelligible to the lay mind. This is theology in its most win-

[17] *Ibid.*, pp. 122-123.
[18] *Ibid.*, pp. 212, 213.

some, enlightening and persuasive expression. This, Mrs. Sayers believes, is what the complicated and obscure phrases of the Athanasian Creed are bent on declaring.

6.

What conclusions, then, can we set down regarding the Christian belief in the Trinity?

We have repeatedly emphasized that the Doctrine of the Trinity as a declaration concerning the inmost being of God takes its rise from the empirical data of a three-fold reception of divine manifestation which is nearly universal in Christian experience, and therefore normative for Christian Faith.

An initial question may be raised whether it is justifiable, let alone mandatory, to read up into the Divine Being Himself distinctions which are indisputably real in men's apprehensions of the Divine Being. So, Schleiermacher. The answer most frequently pressed is that we *must* do so, for at least two reasons:

1. To refuse to do so is to be condemned to remain forever in the realm of the merely phenomenal, the human, the subjective. This is an unsound rejoinder, and it is important to see clearly why it is unsound. Thus far, we have contrasted two terms—the TRINITY OF EXPERIENCE and the TRINITY OF SPECULATION. But there is a third, an intermediary term of highest consequence—the TRINITY OF REVELATION. Recognition of the Christian Trinity is not merely a description of human experience; it is an assertion of Divine Manifestation. It is not just a report of what men feel or think. It is a declaration concerning God, how God wills to make Himself known to men. It is an affirmation of Revelation, and

Revelation is not merely subjective; it is a disclosure of the truth of objective Reality. Therefore it is, in the strictest sense, an affirmation of theology.

2. But, it is argued, the Christian mind cannot rest satisfied simply with a statement of God's disclosure of Himself. It cannot escape the inner necessity of inquiring what light His Revelation of Himself casts upon His inmost Being, what our assured knowledge of God's gracious self-manifestation to us implies regarding what God is in Himself. However, there appears to be wide variation in what are termed "the necessities of human thought" in this particular. Here would seem to lie the heart of a real difference between the characteristic Eastern and Western Christian minds—the degree to which they feel speculative compulsion.

A sounder as well as more modest answer to the query whether we should attempt to go beyond the TRINITY OF REVELATION to the TRINITY OF SPECULATION would appear to be: We rightly yearn to know as much regarding God as it is possible for the Christian mind to learn. Therefore, it is entirely appropriate that we should inquire whether God's three-fold manifestation of Himself tells us anything as to what God is in His inmost being; and, if so, what. But it also reminds us of the purely speculative and hypothetical character of our conclusions.

We have seen that, at every stage of Trinitarian formulation from the Third Century to the present day, speculation regarding the inner Being of the Godhead has moved along two alternative lines:

1. Analogy from men's relations with each other to relations within the Divine Being.

2. Analogy from individual human consciousness to the inmost character of the Divine consciousness, justified by the basic recognition that "man is made in the image of God."

These two alternative lines spring respectively from concern for the three-fold manifestation of God, *and* from concern for the unity of God.

Let us reappraise these two methods:

1. Is it possible to think of the Divine Being as a society of Divine Persons, analogous to a society of human persons? This was the attempt of the Cappadocians with their somewhat crude analogy of Peter, James and John. It seems to be implied in Augustine's third figure of Lover, Beloved, Love. It is suggested, though disavowed, in Barth's triad of Revealer, Revealed, Revealedness. It is vigorously advocated by speculative disciples of the modern social emphasis. It is ably defended today by such Anglican theologians as Canon Hodgson.

The answer is: It *is* possible so to think of the Godhead. Let us attempt a fresh illustration. Let us imagine triplets, as alike as the proverbial "three peas in a pod"—born of the same lineage, possessing identical equipments of mind and heart and will, so intimately akin that they think alike and feel alike and desire alike in all respects and at every moment. Let us suppose that they are wholly one in purpose, together bent on the united realization of the same great Design; let us say, the prosecution of a military campaign. But, the more effectively to accomplish their common End, they agree upon a division of responsibility. One is assigned the role of Chief-of-Staff, remaining at headquarters, in continuous contact at all times with his brothers on the field of battle, and at all points in complete harmony of thought and plan with them. The second brother is given the task of Commander of the Vanguard, a special assignment within their total Plan of Battle, but one of supreme importance. The third brother holds a roving commission, Liaison-man, moving freely over the whole field, maintaining contact between his two brothers and their widely dispersed forces, and even penetrating the ranks of the enemy to seek to win them to the great objective.

It *is* possible to think of three persons, even human persons, thus one.

Now, alter the terms of reference. Substitute, as the End in view, for the winning of a military compaign, the winning of mankind into partnership in the Divine Purpose and into fellowship with the Divine Reality; substitute, for three brothers, joint military commandants, three persons of the single gracious redemptive Godhead. We have a suggestion of how we might conceive the Divine Trinity in such fashion. The great question is: Are we justified in hypothesizing some such community of Persons within the Godhead, and is it necessary to do so? The values of so thinking of God are its stimulus to imagination, its enrichment of our always inadequate and earth-bound thoughts of the ineffable and inexhaustible Deity. Its danger is that, even with the best safeguards, we think of three Gods, not one God; that is to say, it tends toward tritheism.

2. And the alternative method—analogy from human consciousness to the Divine Consciousness? This was the favorite line of reasoning of Augustine, of Western theologians generally, of Hegel. We can hardly imagine a more stimulating and persuasive development of it than that of Mrs. Sayers. It is suggestive of the richness of the Divine

Nature and His experience—the diversities of expression possible within a single consciousness. Its danger is a too literal application of a too limited analogy.

Is there still a third candidate for the method of analogy? I believe there is; and one which, so far as I am aware, has never been adequately exploited and attempted in the schools of theology. It is the analogy of an individual human person in three aspects of his self-expression, in three functions and sets of relationships.

Dr. Fosdick, I believe it was, who employed this analogy, in seeking to make the Christian Trinity intelligible and meaningful, not to theological pundits, or to "grass-roots" preachers, but to American schoolboys. He took, as his illustration, Theodore Roosevelt. There were at least three ways in which Theodore Roosevelt could be, and was in fact, known by his contemporaries; there are at least three avenues which anyone today desiring to comprehend that rich and dynamic person in his fullness must follow; there are three contrasted sources of understanding of him on the basis of his own self-disclosure in his writings. The separate avenues seem to lead to three persons, three Theodore Roosevelts. And so it will appear unless one recognizes that he is being introduced, not to three persons, but to one person in three aspects.

In the first place, there was Theodore Roosevelt—the public figure, the politician, the statesman, the president of the Republic. All of us have seen photographs of him, in long black frock coat, stern eyes staring sharply through eyeglasses—severe, aloof, austere—as he unfailingly seemed to those who called on him in the presidential office or knew him only in official relationships. That Roosevelt is portrayed by his own pen in his *Autobiography*.

And there was also Theodore Roosevelt—the sportsman, the huntsman, the military campaigner, the explorer—a robust, tough, virile man-among-men—seeking the recovery of physical health on the Western plains, leading his Rough Riders up San Juan Hill, stalking big game in the Amazon or African wilds. If you would be introduced to *that* Roosevelt by himself, read his *The Winning of the West*.

But there was a third Theodore Roosevelt, known to few, but with what precious memories and in what contrast to either the forbidding statesman or the rough plainsman—gentle, winsome, boyish, incurably mischievous playmate of the young, burrowing his nose into the great rug before the open hearth of his loved retreat at Sagamore Hill, Oyster Bay, in some wild frolic. If you would meet him, turn to his *Letters to His Children*.

Which was the true Theodore Roosevelt? One might have thought he knew well one of these "persons" and never suspected that there was another, two others. The three avenues of acquaintance lead to three different Theodore Roosevelts; no, not "three persons," but one person in three separate "modes of operation."

If this can be true of almost any finite person—and a hundred others might be substituted—how much more of the Infinite Person, the Living God.

In summary, in our attempts to comprehend, even though inadequately, the Being of God, we are on right lines to employ the method of human analogy, anthropomorphism, reading God's nature in terms drawn from human experience at its noblest, both because this is a sound corollary of our basic certitude that "man is made in the image of God" and is supported by the authority of Jesus' unfailing practice and repeated injunction ("if you, being evil, know how to give good gifts to your children, how much more your Father in Heaven") ; and also because we have no other way to think when we try to conceive God. But our analogies should be drawn, not from a multiplicity of persons, not from the distinction of faculties or functions within each person, but from the familiar reality of the measureless variety and richness of a single whole person in his manifold experience and expression.

7.

How, then, shall we conceive the relationship of God—as Father, as Son, and as Holy Spirit?

It is a relation—not of separation, but of interdependence. All three are affirmations concerning God. Strictly speaking, they must properly be thought always *together,* never separately:

GOD THE FATHER stresses the ultimacy of the Divine. The certainty of God's existence—His Infinity, His Eternity, His Power—we may know from this vast and mysterious Creation in which our lives are set, which speaks to us ever of THE CREATOR AND SUSTAINER OF ALL THAT IS—"God, the Father Almighty, Maker of Heaven and Earth."

Ultimacy affirms the transcendence of God. It reminds us of the mystery, the ineffability, as well as the primacy and finality of Deity. Here, we think of God primarily in His relation to the whole of His Creation.

JESUS CHRIST defines the character of God and of His Holy Spirit. The character of that Being in whom we must believe, we discern in the face of Jesus Christ—His mind, His life, His faith. That mighty, limitless Ultimate Power is not mere undifferentiated Might; but the life-transforming, life-re-deeming Energy of the character of Jesus of Nazareth. In and through Christ, we discern the nature of His Purposes and the manner of His working for their realization. But that character known in Christ is omnipotent—of immeasurable and wholly adequate resource for every necessity. JESUS CHRIST speaks of God's Redeeming Work for and upon man. Here, we have in view primarily God's relation to mankind —to each man and to all in the tale of human history.

THE HOLY SPIRIT affirms the intimacy of omnipotent Power discerned as to His character in Jesus Christ. The never-failing availability of that Power—His ready accessibility to each of us at every moment, of this the HOLY SPIRIT testifies. But that intimate Presence is not some ghostly, mystifying specter; but the actual spirit of Jesus of Nazareth, now immediately present and yet the very Being of Ultimate Reality. The HOLY SPIRIT declares God's omnipresence. Here, we think especially of God-near and God-at-work in the souls of those ready and eager to receive Him.

We see that each—Father, Son, Holy Spirit—enlarges, qualifies, enriches our understanding of each of the others.

8.

Lastly, then, how shall we think of God?

To say the same again, but in different fashion:

THE EXISTENCE OF GOD, HIS POWER—we know through His Creation; for, "In the beginning, He created the Heavens and the Earth." But, that POWER which rules the stars in their courses—that very self-same POWER—is, quite literally, closer than breathing, nearer than hands and feet—a Presence more accessible and more intimate than our dearest; and, that POWER is, in His inmost Being, the same goodness and love and loveliness seen so clearly in Jesus of Nazareth—the GOD AND FATHER OF JESUS CHRIST.

THE CHARACTER OF GOD—we discern in Jesus Christ. For "God who commanded the light to shine out of darkness hath shined in our hearts, to give the light of the knowledge of the glory of God in the face of Jesus Christ." That CHARACTER, so clearly, so compellingly, so irresistibly clamant upon our affection and loyalty and trust—JESUS CHRIST— that very self-same CHARACTER is, quite literally, the Sovereign of Creation, the Ruler of the Universe, the Ultimate Power which determines all; and, that CHARACTER in all His Infinite Power and Infinite Grace is the nearest, dearest Companion of our solicitude and our yearning.

THE NEVER-FAILING AVAILABILITY OF GOD—of this, we are made sure in the Holy Spirit. But, that PRESENCE—so near, so intimate, ever about us and within us—that very self-same PRESENCE pervades the whole Universe, and determines its every atom and motion; and, that PRESENCE, often so hauntingly vague and mysterious, is—the Spirit of Jesus Christ.

So, we may declare:—"I believe—in God, the Father Almighty, Maker of heaven and earth; and—in Jesus Christ, His Son, our Lord; and—in the Holy Spirit, which is the Spirit of Christ, which is the Spirit of God."

"THE GRACE OF THE LORD JESUS CHRIST, AND THE LOVE OF GOD, AND THE FELLOWSHIP OF HIS HOLY SPIRIT—be with us all."

INDEX

Acts, Book of, 57 ff.
Alexandria, 48 f.
Alexandria, School of, 109
Allen, A. V. G., 83 n.
Amos, 39, 79
Anabaptism, 82 f., 134
Anglicanism, 133
Anglo-Catholicism, 128 f., 137 f.
animism, 35
anthropomorphism, 118 ff., 156 ff.
Antioch, School of, 109
Apocrypha, 47
Apostles' Creed, 4, 73
Apostolic Fathers, 74
Aristides, 74
Athanasian Creed, 3 f., 159, 169
Augustine, 77, 129, 157 ff., 162, 168, 171
authority, 90

Baillie, D. M., 109, 166
baptism, 134
Barth, Karl, 164 f., 171
Basil, 153 ff.
Brethren, 134
Brown, William Adams, 12
Brunner, Emil, 97 ff.
Buchmanism, ix, 136 n.
Buddhism, 23 ff.
"Buddhist-Christian Institute, The," 23 ff.

Calvin, 80 ff., 130 ff.
Calvinism, 133
Cappadocian Fathers, 153 ff., 161, 163 f., 171
categorical imperative, 97
Catholicism, 84, 90, 91, 125
"Chosen People," 41, 50
Christian Hope, 11
Christian Unity, 68
Christianity and Buddhism, 23 ff.
Christianity and other religions, 17, 20, 84, 91, 92
Christo-centric theology, 4, 136
Church, 12, 27, 41, 67 ff., 123 f., 130 ff., 134 f.
Church union, 124
Classic Protestantism, 80 ff., 90, 91, 127 ff., 130 ff., 144
communion of spirit, 111

Congregationalism, 82 ff., 134
conscience, 90
Council of Chalcedon, 108
Council of Constantinople, 76, 108
Council of Nicaea, 73, 76, 107 f.
Council of Trent, 80, 129
Craig, Clarence Tucker, 11 n.
Creation, 34, 44, 48, 50, 95 f., 176
christology, 71 ff.

David, 37, 54
Davidson, A. B., 39 n.
Dead Sea Scrolls, 48 n.
Deism, 117 f.
Dillistone, F. W., 144 n.
Disciples of Christ, 83, 134

Early Church, 41, 57 ff., 125, 156
Eastern Christendom, 76
Eastern Orthodoxy, 91
ecstasy, 59, 65
Ecumenical Movement, 122, 139
Edinburgh Conference of 1937, 123
Edwards, D. Miall, 110 n.
Edwards, Jonathan, 82 f.
Egyptian religion, 152
Elijah, 37 f.
Enoch, 48
episcopacy, 78, 129
Epistle of Barnabas, 74
Essenes, 48 n.
Eucharist, 39
Ezekiel, 40, 42 f., 48

First Epistle of Clement, 74
Fitch, Albert Parker, xii
forgiveness, 103
Fosdick, H. E., 173 f.
"Free Churches," 82 f.
freedom, 101 f., 144
Friends, viii, 17, 40, 82, 134, 136
friendship, 111
Fulton, W., 151 n.

Gideon, 37
glossolalia, 59
God, ix, 3 f., 15 f., 17 f., 91, 101, Ch. 7, 123, 166 ff., 175 ff. (see also, Spirit of God)
God's Will, 100
Gore, Charles, 14 n., 138 n.